BARNARD CASTLE

LIST OF SUBSCRIBERS
to the hardback edition

Mr & Mrs S G Abbott
Mrs Irene Adamson
Mr G L H Alderson
Mr & Mrs E W & K M Allinson
Mrs M I Appleby (*née* Huck)
Mr & Mrs T G & M Ashburner (2 copies)
Mrs M E Atkinson
Mr S Atkinson

Mrs F I Bainbridge
Mr H Bainbridge
Mr P Ball
Mr M H Balshaw
Mr & Mrs R P Banks
Mr & Mrs A M Barmby
Barnard Castle School
Mr E & Mrs S Barnes
Miss D A Batey
Mr & Mrs I R Baxter
Mr A Beadle
Bede Day Centre
Mr M Bell
Mr R A Bell
Dr & Mrs D N Bentley
Mr & Mrs B J Biddiscombe
Dr & Mrs A E Biggin
Dr & Mrs M S Biggs
Mr & Mrs D M P Blakely
Mr & Mrs B W Blouet
Dr & Mrs G M Bolton
Mr T A Boothroyd
Mr & Mrs G L Bousfield
Mrs E Bowman
Mrs H E Brass
Mr S W Bray
Mrs M R La Brie
Mr & Mrs D A Briggs
Mr & Mrs C A Brown
Mr & Mrs D J Brown
K & M O Brown
Mr J B Browne
The Rev & Mrs J B Browne
Mr & Mrs K & M Brunton
Miss R J Brunton
Kevin Burnley
Mr & Mrs R S Burns
Mr J V Burroughs
Mr & Mrs G L Busfield

Dr & Mrs F G Buttler
Mr & Mrs G C Bywater

Mr & Mrs D Caig
Colonel & Mrs K D Calder
Mr & Mrs G A Camozzi
Mr & Mrs K C R Campbell
Mr A J Carr
Mr & Mrs G Carr
Mr I G Carr
Mr M N Carr
Miss R E Carr
Mr B Carter
Mr C E Carter
Mrs Vera Chapman
Mr & Mrs H Charlesworth
Mrs K Chesman
Mr & Mrs R Child
Mr & Mrs P G Chrisp
Mrs A M Chubb
Sqn Ldr RAF (rtd) W T Clapperton
Rev M W & Mrs D Clark
Miss F Clarke
Mr & Mrs J A Collings
Mr W Collinson
Mr & Mrs J A Cook
Mr B Copland
Mr Michael Thomas Craig
Mr L & Mrs J Crossling
Mr N J Crowther
Mr S J Crowther
Mr & Mrs J S Cutler

Mrs J S Davidson
Mrs G E Davies
Mr & Mrs F Davis
Mr & Mrs J Davison
Mrs E C Day
Mr & Mrs T Dent
Miss T A Dickinson
Mr A M M Dixon (2 copies)
Mr & Mrs E Dixon
Mrs P M Dixon
Mr J Donaldson
Mr K Dougherty
Mr & Mrs S C Doyle
Mr D Dresser
Mr M J Dry

Mr P H Dry
Mr S M Dry
Mr N I Dugdale
Michael & Judy Dunsmore

Mr & Mrs P Eaves
Mrs C B Edwards
Mr I R Edwards
Mr J Edwards
Mr & Mrs R D Edwards
Mr & Mrs G C Elliott
Miss L E Elliott
Miss N Elliott
Mr & Mrs R & K Elliott
Dr D J Evans
Mr & Mrs D C S Everall
Mr & Mrs J S Evered

Mr & Mrs J S Faichney
Dr K J Fairless
Mr & Mrs W R Farrer
Mrs S O Ferguson
Ms A Fine
Mrs S Finlay
Mr & Mrs J R Forrest
A Forster
Miss D Forster
J E Forster
Mr & Mrs N W Foster
Mr & Mrs R D Foster
Mr & Mrs M R Foulston
Tom Fowke

Mrs E Gartland
Mr & Mrs M & E A Gaskin
Mrs M Gibbs
Miss M Gilson
Mr & Mrs I M Goldsack
Mr & Mrs S J Goldsack
Mrs E Gott
Mrs J M Gray
Mr S W Gray
Mr & Mrs P W Greenhalgh
Ms R C Greenhalgh
Mr & Mrs J K Gregory
Mr & Mrs W A Greig
Mrs P Gunderman

Mr & Mrs J C Hammond
Mrs J M Hanby
Mr & Mrs Hardie-Hammond
Mr & Mrs A J Harding
Mr & Mrs E E Hardy

Mr A S D Harris
Mr D W G Harris
Miss F M Hatchell
Mrs L D Headlam-Morley
Miss J Hedley
Mr & Mrs M J Hemingway
Mr & Mrs J T Henderson
Mrs P Henshaw
Mr & Mrs J B Hetherington
Mrs M Heywood
Mr & Mrs B Higgins
Mrs J M Hillery Robinson
Mr R E (Ted) Hinchcliffe
Mrs J F P Hodgson
Mr & Mrs M T Hodgson
Mr & Mrs B D Holmes
Mr & Mrs E Hornby

Mrs & Mrs C F & T Irwin

Mr N & Mrs E Jackson
Mr & Mrs A Jameson
Miss R M Jenkins
Rev Mr J D Johns
Mr & Mrs C P Johnson
Mrs J Johnson (2 copies)
Mrs M Johnson
Mrs J R Johnston
Mr A Jones
Mr D Jones
Mrs E Jones
Mr & Mrs J A Jones
Mr & Mrs P D Jones
Mr & Mrs R T L Jones
Mr & Mrs R W Jones
Mrs E A Jopling
Mr & Mrs R F Jopling

Mr & Mrs F W Keighley
Mr & Mrs J L Keighley
Mr P & Mrs J Kelly
Mr P J Kent
Mr K C N G King
Mr & Mrs C A Kipling
Mr R Kirby
Mr & Mrs D J Kirk
Mr & Mrs D R Kneller
Mrs E Knight
John Knights
Mr & Mrs J A Knox
Mr & Mrs D Kyle
Mr & Mrs D D Kyle
Mr & Mrs P J Kirkman

Dr A G Leishman
Mr F J Leishman
Mrs R Lette
Mrs & Mrs A Liddle
Mr & Mrs C I Lincoln
Charles Henry Littlefair
Mr & Mrs M S Lowe
Mrs J L Lowes
Miss M Lowes
Mr M D Lowes
Mrs & Mrs J Lowson
Mr A Lowther
Mr Frederick Lucas
Douglas & Myra Lycett (2 copies)
Mrs K Lynn

Mr R T McAndrew
Mr & Mrs D McKitton
Mr & Mrs B W McMurray
Mr & Mrs G McNeil
Mr E Mackie
Mr & Mrs A R Magson
Mr & Mrs A W A Maisey
Mr & Mrs W M Maisey
Mr & Mrs S G Markham
Mr & Mrs D M Marshall
Mrs M Mattison
Mr & Mrs A J Maude
Mr & Mrs J K Mayberry
Mr & Mrs R J Mead
Mrs D M Metcalf
Barry and Jacqueline Metcalfe
Mr R G Millard
Miss M Milner
Miss V A Musto
Mrs B Mitchell
Prof & Mrs David M Moore
Rev & Mrs J A Moore
Mr R W Moore
Mr & Mrs M J S Moss
Mr & Mrs K F Mould
Mr & Mrs D B Mounter
Mr & Mrs M Mumford
Mr J M Musto
Mr M T Musto
Miss V A Musto

Dr & Mrs J C Nainby-Luxmoore
Mr & Mrs G Newbiggin
Mr & Mrs D & J A Nicholson
Mrs Ann Nicholson
Mr & Mrs W P Nicholson
Miss C J Normington

Mr & Mrs P Normington
Mr & Mrs I Nuttall

Mr & Mrs J O'Hern
Mr J S O Olaman
Mr J M Outhwaite

Mr D G Parkin
Mr & Mrs G C Parkin
Mr H C Parr
Mr & Mrs W B Peat
Mr I S Petherick
Mr P J Phillips (3 copies)
Mr J C Pickering
Mr O S Pickering
Dr & Mrs K H Pickworth
Professor A J Pollard
Mrs A Porter
Mrs J Priestley
Miss C Prince
Mr & Mrs O S Purvis
Mr S Purvis
Canon A Pyburn

Mr & Mrs A A Railton (2 copies)
Mr F P Raine
Mrs K J Ranner
Mr T C Raw
Mr & Mrs G A Redfearn (2 copies)
Mr R Redfearn
Mrs M E Reed
Mrs F D Rhodes
Miss B M C Richards
Mrs Margaret A Rigby (*née* Dodgson)
Mrs Julia Roberts
Mr & Mrs K N Robinson
Mr & Mrs D Robson
Mr & Mrs D M & A Robson
Mr & Mrs K W Rowland
Mr & Mrs M J Rutter

Mr W J C Sager
Mr C Sanderson
Mr & Mrs K Sanderson
Mrs P M Scrafton
Mr A J Seaman
Mr & Mrs C J G Severs
Mr & Mrs R H Siswick
Geoff Smith
Mr & Mrs J T Smith
Mrs M E Sowerby
Mr D A Sparrow
Mr J G Sparrow

Mr & Mrs S Spencer
Mr & Mrs D R Spiby
Miss Betty Stammer
Mr & Mrs T A Stamp
Mr & Mrs P W Stanger
Mr & Mrs C Stephenson
Mr & Mrs M J Sutter
Mr R Symonds

Mrs G Tallentire
Mr W L Tallentire
Mr C Tarn
Miss S A Tarn
Mr & Mrs D Tavendale
Mrs L Taylor
Mrs K Teward
Mr & Mrs R Thistlethwaite
Mrs J Thompson
Mr & Mrs M W & G Thwaites
Mr & Mrs D R Toes
Mrs L Tomlinson
Mr & Mrs H A Travis
Mr & Mrs D Trow
Mr & Mrs W B Tucker
Mrs D I Tunstall
Mr & Mrs P & J Turner
Mr & Mrs J H Turrell
Mr & Mrs R A Twinn
Dr M P K Twomey

Mr J B Vallack

Amy Waddell
Andrew Waddell
Mr & Mrs G A Walker
Mrs Joan Walker
Mr & Mrs M Walker
Mrs J Wallis
Mr & Mrs M Warriner
Mr J P Watson
Mrs S Webster
Mr R Wilkinson
Mr Jim Wilson
Mr K Wilson
Mr M V Wilson
Mr V Wilson
Mr & Mrs M J Winsor
Mr & Mrs A S Wood
Miss H J Wood
Mr & Mrs J H Wood
Mrs S Wood
Dr W R Wooff, OBE
Mr F J Wright
Mr & Mrs L G W Wright

Lt Col & Mrs T D Yeats
Dr William Yellowley
Mr & Mrs C Young

LIST OF SUBSCRIBERS
to the paperback edition

Mrs D Ainslie
Mrs R S Allen
Miss C M Allinson
Mr & Mrs J J Allinson
Mr & Mrs W A Ashley

Mrs P A Barker
Miss E Barnes
Mr & Mrs W J Bartle
Mrs M J Bell
Mrs J E Black
Mr & Mrs D I Blackett
Professor & Mrs H Bowen-Jones
Mr & Mrs P Bowman
Mrs H E Brass
Mr R J T Brown

Mr J B Browne
The Rev & Mrs J B Browne

Mr B Capstick
Mr & Mrs J D Carlisle
Mr & Mrs D W Carmichael
Mr M Churms
Miss F Clarke
Mrs H M Cloutt
Mrs C A Colenutt
Mrs E M Conran
Mr M F Cowling
Mr & Mrs R J Coysh

Mrs M A Dant
Mr & Mrs John A R Davis

Mr P Dixon
Mr & Mrs S Dixon

Mr & Mrs E C Eden
Rev R H & Mrs J Ellis
Mr & Mrs J S Evered

Ms A Fine (2 copies)
Mr & Mrs B Firth
Ms J M Fisher
Mrs R M Francis

Miss D M Gibson
Mr & Mrs R M Gibson
Mr & Mrs S J Goldsack
Mr & Mrs I M Goldsack
Mrs C M Greenwood
Mr & Mrs E W Gregory
Mr J W Gritton
Mrs P Gunderman
Mr B C Guy
Mr N G Guy
Mr T M Guy

Mr & Mrs C B Harrison
Mr & Mrs W Hatton
Mr & Mrs P N Heron
Ms J Hodgson

Mr & Mrs B & M Ingham

Mrs E L Jackson
Mr & Mrs J B Jennings
Mr & Mrs J A Johnson

Major & Mrs G L Kavanagh
Mr & Mrs P J Kirkman

Mr & Mrs B Land
Dr N Land
Mr D N Lee
Miss E B S Leishman
Mrs R Lette
Mrs M F Little
Mrs M D Lodge
Mrs J L Lowes
Mr G R Lowson
Mr A Lowther

Mr & Mrs A R Magson
Mr & Mrs A & M Marr
Mr & Mrs W M & J O Marshall

Mr & Mrs E P Mason (3 copies)
Rev M J Melia
Miss W Melville
Mr & Mrs D I Metcalf
Mr & Mrs V & F Mexter
Mr R W Moore
Miss D Mudd

Miss M Nicholson

Mr & Mrs W E Pankhurst
Dr R B Parkinson
Mr N J Philbey
Mrs J Philipson
Mr & Mrs D J Pittuck

Mr & Mrs C Ridsdale
Mrs I Ridsdale
Mrs M G Rodwell
Mr I T A Rogers
Mr M G Rogers

Mr W J C Sager
Mr A W Scott
Mr & Mrs A Sergeant
Mr & Mrs M F Sharratt
Mrs C G Simpson
Cherry Simpson
Mr George Stastny
Mr & Mrs C Stephenson
Mr J Stevens

Mr & Mrs D A Teasdale
Mr & Mrs J W Thompson
Mrs E Todd
Mrs L Tomlinson
Mr & Mrs R J & F M M (Richard and
    Fiona) Turnbull
Mr & Mrs A Turner
Mr & Mrs David Turner
Mr Denis Turner
Dr M P K Twomey

Mrs P M Walton
Mr & Mrs M Warriner
Mr Eric Weaver
Mrs L M White
Mr & Mrs John Whitworth
Mrs M M Wilson
Mrs M Wright (3 copies)

Dr William Yellowley

LIST OF SUBSCRIBERS
to the deluxe edition

1	Denise and Ken Smith
2	Mr P and Mrs G Murray
3	Mr Alan Wilkinson
4	Teesdale District Council
5	Mark R Whitley
6	Mr & Mrs S Hope-Robertson
7	Miss T Myers
8	Miss H M Smith
9	Mr M Gasson
10	Mr P and Mrs C McCann
11	Mr M R Elder
12	Miss F Clarke
13	Mr C J Higgins
14	Mrs Isylaine Edwards
15	Mr & Mrs M Hawkins
16	Mr W J Cummins
17	Mrs June Carter
18	Mr G H Metcalfe
19	Mr A Metcalfe
20	Mrs G Almond
21	Mr V Walker
22	Mrs N A Atkinson
23	Mrs M Hyde
24	Mr J A Gibson
25	Mr G J Holmes
26	Mr & Mrs R E Bland
27	Mr & Mrs D I Metcalf
28	Mrs K Gaskarth
29	Miss S L Land
30	Mr & Mrs R C Brown
31	Mrs M H French
32	Mrs C Wallace
33	Mr & Mrs L Townsend
34	Mrs P D Snedden
35	Mr & Mrs G D Jameson
36	Mr & Mrs S Hatton
37	Mr J E Rhodes
38	Mr A J Betterton
39	Mr & Mrs W K Wherry
40	Mr H A Higginbottom
41	Mr & Mrs B Davies
42	Mrs J Clarke
43	Dr T J & Mrs L Morse
44	Miss M I Hillery
45	Mr & Mrs J Bloomfield
46	Mr & Mrs W M Maisey
47	Dr C & Mrs V F Burgess
48	Mr R J A Burgess
49	Miss C R C Burgess
50	Miss V J E Burgess
51	Mr & Mrs J G Worsnop
52	Mrs N J Lobley
53	Mr A J Renham
54	Dr W F Heyes
55	Mr & Mrs John Whitworth
56	Mr & Mrs K M Everitt
57	Mr & Mrs J P Wilkinson
58	Mr K Emberton
59	Mr & Mrs J A Liverseed
60	Mr & Mrs J D Hodgson
61	Mrs J M Hillery Robinson
62	Mr Michael A Harris
63	Mrs J H Moss-Smith
64	Dr S R Jones
65	Miss J Ainsley
66	Mrs K N Higginbottom
67	Mr J L Reed
68	Mr & Mrs B Garnett
69	Mr P J Atkinson
70	Subscribed
71	Miss A Dineley
72	Mr & Mrs R G Embleton
73	Mr & Mrs G O Solomon
74	Mr Frederick Stanley Chape
75	Dr & Mrs D S Dry
76	Mr & Mrs F P Murton
77	Mr & Mrs M F N & H A Courtley
78	Mr & Mrs J M Audas
79	Mr G Burton
80	Lea and Keon Tan
81	Barnard Castle School
82	Mr & Mrs J S Crowther
83	Mrs N Goodson
84	Mr G Ian Goodson
85	Mr J R Watson
86	Joyce Ann Lawton
87	Peter & Janine McNair
88	Stephen K Sowerby
89	Mr & Mrs P J Cody
90	Mr & Mrs R W Knight
91	Mr R A Howe

92	Mr & Mrs E W Davey	102	Mr James Anthony Elliott
93	Mrs L E Butterworth	103	Mrs S Walton
94	Mr & Mrs A Davies	104	Mr P J Phillips
95	G Donald Smith	105	Joseph P Barker
96	Mr & Mrs N J Watson	106	Miss T A Dickinson
97	Mrs G Hugill	107	Mrs A M Tarn
98	Mrs G Hugill	108	Mr & Mrs J Fawcett
99	Mrs G Hugill	109	Subscribed
100	Mr & Mrs P Hughes	110	Mr H H Wright
101	Mr D A Helliwell	111	Mr C A R Ruckley

BARNARD CASTLE
Historic Market Town

Alan Wilkinson

SMITH SETTLE
1998

First published in 1998 by
Smith Settle Ltd
Ilkley Road
Otley
West Yorkshire
LS21 3JP

ISBN   Paperback   1 85825 095 1
        Hardback   1 85825 096 X

British Library Cataloguing-in-Publication data:
A catalogue record for this book is available from the British Library.

Set in Monotype Plantin.

Designed, printed and bound by
SMITH SETTLE
Ilkley Road, Otley, West Yorkshire LS21 3JP

Contents

Acknowledgements

Many people have helped in preparing this book. Thanks are due to members of staff at the Barnard Castle Branch of Durham County Library; The Bowes Museum, Barnard Castle; the Darlington Library Centre for Local Studies; the Durham County Record Office; the Durham Light Infantry Museum; and the Planning Department of Teesdale District Council.

Copyright photographs have been reproduced from the collections of the following: Airviews (Manchester) Ltd, pages 123 and 125; Beamish North of England Open Air Museum, Stanley, County Durham, pages 82, 83 and 106; the Bowes Museum, Barnard Castle, pages 43, 58, 89, 92 (top), 96 (top), 97, 103, 109 (bottom) and 124; the Durham Light Infantry Museum, Aykley Heads, Durham, pages 107 and 108; *Teesdale Mercury*, Barnard Castle, page 131; and Mr Alan Curtis, Scarborough, pages 5 (top) and 34.

The map on page 136 is based upon Ordnance Survey material with the permission of the Controller of Her Majesty's Stationery Office, © Crown Copyright Licence No MC85365M, and with the consent of Teesdale District Council whose officers added later details.

For providing some of the other illustrations, I am indebted to Mr Gordon Lincoln, Mr Jim Morrow, Mr Lance Nelson and Mr Parkin Raine. Other local residents have provided information by supplying books and documents, or inviting me to see interesting internal features of their historic houses or business premises. In particular I record my gratitude to Mr Edgar Dixon and the late Mr Cyril Walker for comments and information based on their long experience of local government in Barnard Castle, and for giving me access to significant documents.

I am grateful to members of my family for their help: my son, Andrew, and my daughter, Amanda Hodgson, supplied photographs; my son-in-law, Philip Hodgson, created the five original maps (pages 7, 8, 66, 74 and 100); my daughter, Diana Everall, made useful suggestions on earlier versions of the book, and my son, Matthew, did a substantial amount of typing.

Finally, I thank my wife, Jean, for her painstaking work and valuable comments which considerably improved the final text.

Alan Wilkinson
Barnard Castle

Earth, rolling down the slopes of the dry moat of the castle, has almost blocked the archway of the fourteenth century sally port. Originally a mounted man could ride through it to guard the bridge.

I

Early Years
1100–1600

On a grassy ridge, about two miles (3km) north of Barnard Castle, an apparently haphazard arrangement of stones lies embedded in the turf. In this peaceful area of Teesdale, in the south-western corner of County Durham, lapwings and curlews call overhead while sheep and rabbits graze among the old grey stones — which is all that now remains of the vanished medieval village of Marwood.

It was a compact village in an enviable situation, but early in the twelfth century its inhabitants often looked anxiously down into the valley of the River Tees. Their gaze was concentrated on a point where the wooded slopes which stretched below them ended in a high rocky outcrop overlooking the river. On this promontory an aristocratic Frenchman had given instructions to build a castle which was to lead to the virtual disappearance of Marwood and the creation of the market town of Barnard Castle.

The view of the bridge seen from the wall above the sally port of the castle.

The remains of the vanished village of Marwood.

The Frenchman was called Guy de Baliol, a supporter of King William II of England, and the king had granted him a portion of land from which he was expected to exercise control over a large area of northern England on behalf of the king himself. Guy chose to build his castle, partly as a dwelling, partly as an administrative centre, and partly as a fortress, on the southern boundary of his lands. It stood eighty feet (24m) directly above the River Tees and commanded a view of one of the few important river crossings in the area. A Roman road, linking two camps, had formerly crossed the Tees at this point, and its use had continued in Saxon and later times.

The castle was a wooden structure, protected by the river on one side and a deep ravine on another. The weakest side, where the town's market areas were later to be built, was protected by a man-made ditch, crossed by a bridge which gave access to the main gate of the castle.

The family, their servants and some officials were its first inhabitants, and the little village which grew beside the castle provided homes for the people who attended to their daily needs. The immediate area was favourable for the development of a town: the woodland provided timber; stone was near enough to the surface to be easily quarried; and the riverside land downstream from the castle was suitable for ploughing and grazing, providing not only food but also wool for clothing, and leather for both clothes and harness. The part of this land which was nearest to the castle was the large area called the Demesnes.

The lord of the castle kept this land for his own use, and the villagers worked on it under his command. In return, he granted land to the north and east of the town for the villagers' own use. They were also expected to give their lord military service as required, so some of their time was given over to training for this purpose. An area known as the Flatts, close to the northern wall of the castle, became the parade ground and training area. The village was a close-knit community: the inhabitants served the castle, and the castle offered them protection and gave them a livelihood.

Guy's wooden castle lasted for about twenty years before building began on the same site but in an enlarged, more spectacular and lasting form. Guy's immediate successor was Bernard Baliol, who was followed by his son who bore the same name. From about 1130 onwards, these two men established a stone-built fortress which became known as Bernard's Castle, and the name was also given to the town which grew beside it and which the Baliols governed. The castle walls enclosed an area of over six acres (2.5ha), with the boundary wall running along the edge of what became the Horse Market and the Market Place. Another wall enclosed hunting grounds which extended for two miles (3km) up the valley on the north bank of the Tees. It was at this period that the villagers of Marwood moved into Barnard Castle, and their former lands became part of the feudal lord's hunting grounds, called Marwood Chase. There is a tradition that stone from Marwood village was used in building the growing town of Barnard Castle.

By about 1150 the future town plan was already formed. The old Roman road which now exists as Galgate, one of the town's main streets, ran in a straight line directly into the countryside where the townspeople had been granted agricultural rights by the Baliols. To the north-west, reached by the road called Harmire, lay the Town Moor; to the north-east, beside today's Darlington Road and stretching down to the Westwick road, lay the Town Fields and Town Pasture, and a small piece of land

Barnard Castle stands high on a rocky cliff overlooking an ancient river-crossing.

Modern Galgate follows the straight line of a former Roman road.

called the Little Moor. The Town Fields were sub-divided into four large open fields which could also be reached by the Back Lane (or Back Way) which ran parallel to the main streets of the town. This road also still exists along its original route, and is linked to Galgate and the market streets by side streets and narrow pedestrian passageways.

In the town centre the Horse Market and the Market Place still form a continuous curve which follows the line of the outer wall of the castle and runs down the Bank towards the river. To its east, linked to the street by various narrow lanes, lie the Demesnes.

The castle itself was the dominant feature of the medieval town, partly because of its size but also because the lord of the castle allowed no other buildings to interfere with the townspeople's view of it. The Horse Market and the Market Place had buildings on only one side of the street, facing the market areas and the castle beyond.

Old houses on the Bank. On the right is the Steward's House, altered at roof and ground level. The house with a projecting gable, almost directly below the church tower, is the sixteenth century house known as Blagrave's. *(See pages 17 and 26-27.)*

The Inner Ward of the castle today. Residential and domestic quarters are on the left, in the centre are the windows of the great hall, and the massive round tower stands on the right.

5

This suited the Baliol family's purposes, for it gave them a clear view of the town, in case any attack on the castle came from that side, and also allowed them to keep a close eye on activities in the market areas. This was important because the lord of the castle was also lord of the market, and he controlled not only the weekly markets but also the fairs which were held three times a year at Easter and Whitsuntide for 'pedlary' and on Magdalen Eve (21st July) for horses, sheep and cattle. The Baliols kept the money raised by market tolls and the rent of stalls, and were the controllers of weights and measures and the quality of goods sold in the markets.

The south door of St Mary's Church.

The town church also had a dominant position, standing high above the Demesnes. It was small in comparison with the castle, but much larger than the townspeople's own houses or the inns which stood in the market areas. It was at first a simple rectangular building without aisles until one was added in the second half of the twelfth century. Parts of the old building still exist in the present structure, notably the arched northern arcade and the beautiful Norman south door. These enrichments were provided by the Baliols.

The family soon found itself governing a town as well as a castle. The head of the family was a mesne lord, that is, one who held land directly from the Crown and therefore ranked above other feudal lords. His rule extended to cover civil and criminal legal cases, and to convene a manor court to hear pleas. Stocks, pillory and the gallows were all in use. The stocks stood in the Market Place and the gallows were at the top of Galgate, at its junction with the Harmire road. The gallows gave Galgate its name. There was no doubt about who governed the town, and so that there should be no doubt about the system of government, successive heads of the family issued charters, written on parchment in Latin, and bearing the seal of the Baliols.

The first was issued by the second Bernard Baliol about 1160, addressed to 'all his men and friends, French and English' which suggests that the population of the castle and town was of mixed nationality. The charter refers to a class of townsmen called 'burgesses' who were men of some standing who paid rent for land in money rather than in services. The burgesses cultivated portions of land, often attached to their own houses, like large back gardens, whereas other townsmen had to use the shared land outside the town. The Town Fields were cultivated on the strip system, with the various strips of land often changing hands each year so that no one person continually farmed a good or bad area. The Town Moor was used for rough grazing and, according to the charters, the townspeople were allowed to cut peat from it for fires for warmth and for smoke-curing bacon, and to gather thatching materials and wood for fuel or

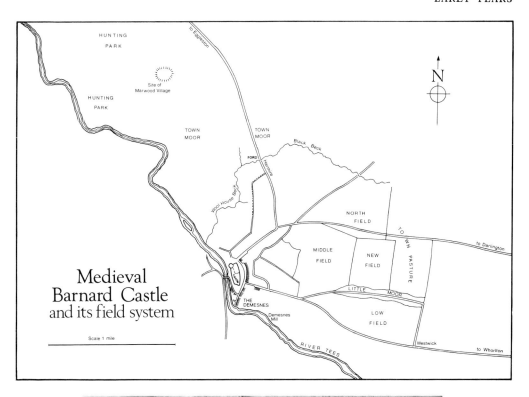

The Baliol seal, attached to the charter of 1250.

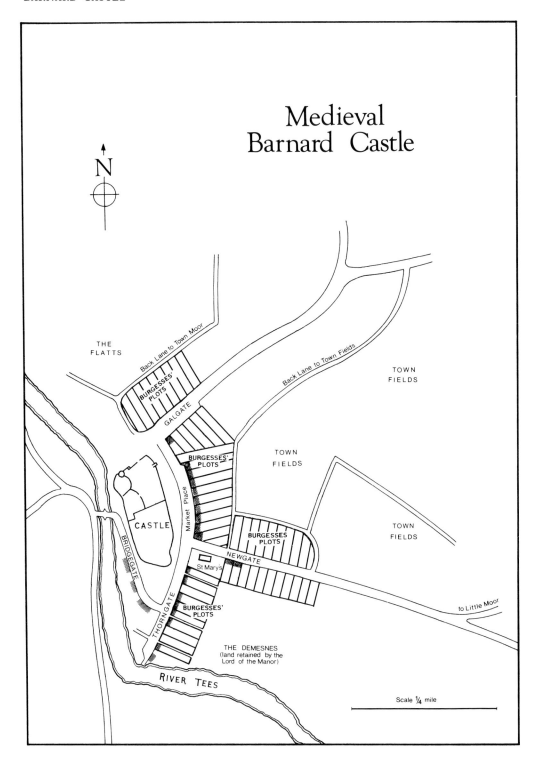

Medieval
Barnard Castle

N

THE
FLATTS

Back Lane to Town Moor

Back Lane to Town Fields

TOWN
FIELDS

BURGESSES'
PLOTS

GALGATE

BURGESSES'
PLOTS

TOWN
FIELDS

Market Place

CASTLE

BURGESSES
PLOTS

TOWN
FIELDS

BRIDGEGATE

NEWGATE

St Mary's

THORNGATE

BURGESSES'
PLOTS

to Little Moor

THE DEMESNES
(land retained by the
Lord of the Manor)

RIVER TEES

Scale ¼ mile

Part of the Town Moor still looks much the same as in medieval days.

building. They were also allowed, without payment, to let their pigs graze in Marwood Chase, eating the acorns and beech nuts.

All these rights were confirmed by charters granted between 1210 and 1270 by successive lords of the castle. Hugh Baliol, who succeeded the second Bernard, was typical of the family in having a liberal and far-sighted attitude to his people. He recognised, for example, that it was in his power to build a communal oven in the town, and then to compel the townspeople to use it and to pay for doing so, but he refrained and freely allowed them to use their own ovens — and he added that if any of his successors did build a town oven, the inhabitants must not be compelled to use it.

Hugh did, however, exercise one monopoly: all people with corn to grind had to use the lord's watermill situated at the foot of his field, the Demesnes. The miller had to be paid his usual fee and the lord was to be given a sixteenth of the corn, or its value. This was quite a fair arrangement, for much of the money would be used to keep the mill in good repair, which was an important consideration as it stood by the fast-flowing River Tees whose water often suddenly rose to a high flood-level.

Hugh hoped that the townspeople would enjoy their privileges 'freely, quietly, and wholly.' John Baliol, who gave the town a charter in 1250, took a similar attitude and named a new class of society called 'freeholders'. It is clear that the Baliols were giving the town a sense of independence which was later to stand the inhabitants in good stead when, eventually, the rule of the Baliols came to an end.

The Baliols were stalwart men who had served their king and country well, and had repulsed various Scottish forays into England during the reigns of King Stephen, King Henry II and King John. In 1228 John Baliol became one of the most influential of the lords of Barnard Castle. His power and influence outstripped his predecessors when he married Devorguilla of Galloway, whose father was constable of Scotland

9

The town's first cornmill stood beside this natural weir on the River Tees, at the foot of the Demesnes.

and whose mother was the niece of King William, the Scottish king. John Baliol thus acquired important estates in Scotland and was related to the royal family. He could be ruthless, too, and ensured his tenancy of the Scottish estates by imprisoning a possible rival claimant, Thomas, the illegitimate son of John's father-in-law, in the castle at Barnard Castle.

John showed his more humane side by founding St John's Hospital in Newgate, Barnard Castle, where thirteen impoverished women were housed and fed under the wardenship of a priest who daily conducted prayers for the founder.

John was also, somewhat indirectly, the founder of Balliol College in Oxford. (The spelling of the family name varied.) In 1254 Bishop Kirkham of Durham imprisoned some of John's retainers who, it was alleged, had committed sacrilege in the church at Long Newton, near Stockton-on-Tees. In reprisal, John took some of the bishop's men and held them in Barnard Castle, for which the bishop banned him from receiving any benefits of the Church. This put matters on a serious level and John Baliol rode to Durham to express his remorse. The Bishop castigated him and, as a penance, ordered him to pay for the lodging and maintenance of six poor scholars at Oxford.

This led to the foundation of Balliol Hall, and when John died in 1269 his widow ensured the future memory of her husband by continuing to maintain the scholars and, in 1282, giving a charter and sufficient money to found Balliol College.

Devorguilla was a devoted wife and widow; after John's death she kept his embalmed heart in an ornamental ivory casket which she set before her on the table at mealtimes. She died in Barnard Castle in 1290, and the casket was taken with her body to Scotland where she was interred with her husband's heart in Sweetheart Abbey, near Dumfries.

John had meanwhile been succeeded by three other Baliols. There was another Hugh (1269-71), followed by Alexander (1271-8), who had no children so was succeeded by his brother, another John (1278-96). This second John acquired more power even than his earlier namesake, whose title of Lord of Galloway he still held. In 1291 the Scottish throne became vacant when the line of succession unexpectedly ceased. There were a dozen claimants to the throne, among whom was John Baliol who based his claim on his relationship, through Devorguilla, to the royal family. (His possible rival, Thomas of Galloway, was enduring his fifty-sixth year of imprisonment in Barnard Castle, so could not present himself as a claimant. Perhaps he did not even know what was happening.)

Before a king was selected, all claimants were warned by King Edward I of England that the successful candidate would have to acknowledge Edward as his over-lord. This was agreed, John Baliol was the successful contender, and he was crowned at Scone on the 30th November 1292. He then found that his promise to Edward I had been no mere formality, for Edward insisted that in any Scottish legal case which went to appeal, the final judgement was to be made by the King of England.

John was not prepared to have his kingship diminished in this way and in 1296 renounced his loyalty to Edward. This led to war and John was defeated at the Battle of Dunbar. Edward compelled him to forfeit the throne of Scotland and all his English lands. This marked the end of all connection between the Baliols and Barnard Castle. John himself was held captive in the Tower of London before being sent as an exile to France, his family's native land, where he lived quietly in his castle in Normandy until his death in 1314.

With the departure of the Baliols, Barnard Castle suddenly found itself without a feudal lord. The shock must have been almost more than we can imagine, for the town had lost its founders and its contemporary organisers. Fortunately the Baliols

The building of St John's Hospital, strengthened and partly rebuilt, survived until 1965.

had given the community a strong sense of independence and, by appointing freemen and burgesses, had imposed social order on the town, but the basis of the medieval system had been lost.

At first the king did nothing about it; nobody was appointed to be lord of Barnard Castle. The gap was filled, on his own initiative and probably without much legal justification, by Anthony Bek, one of the prince bishops of Durham. How much administration he carried out is not clear, but he is reputed to have made additions to the castle buildings and to have taken money from the income of the estate. One man who must have been pleased to see Bishop Bek was Thomas of Galloway, whom the bishop released from the castle after sixty-one years' imprisonment.

After ten years of Bishop Bek's rule Edward I granted the estates to the earl of Warwick. He, too, made additions to the castle and took money from the estates, but generally resided elsewhere in the country.

Barnard Castle itself was a very desirable residence and, except for some areas which were beginning to show signs of neglect, the buildings were completely suitable for administrative and defensive purposes. There was an aristocratic dwelling area which commanded beautiful views up Teesdale, as did the great hall in which banquets and festivities took place, and a tower which contained private chambers reached by an internal staircase with sanitary arrangements at different levels. Other parts of the castle included kitchens, dovecote, bakery, prison, guard rooms, stables, barns, a long chamber for indoor exercise in inclement weather and, within the outermost wall but outside the main buildings, the private chapel and graveyard, beyond which lay the castle's own farm. There was a constable's tower set in a strategic position for administration, and the defences of the castle relied both on its natural situation and a system of moats and protective walls within the castle grounds.

These divided the castle into four separate areas known as 'wards'. The Outer Ward contained the chapel and farm; the Middle Ward contained the storage block, administrative offices, and some living quarters for men and horses; the Town Ward was bounded by the Horse Market, and was protected by a moat and the ravine which ran from the foot of Galgate towards the River Tees. The Town Ward contained the guardrooms and more stables, and gave access to Marwood Chase and the parade grounds. The most secure area of the castle was the Inner Ward which contained the domestic quarters, catering resources, and the huge round Baliol Tower. This was provided with arrow slits placed so that archers could protect the outer walls, and the tower commanded a wide view for it was 70 feet (21m) high and formed, with the cliff on which it stood, a vantage point 150 feet (45m) above the river. Below it, on the outer side, a wall sealed off the lower end of the ravine along which attackers might otherwise have tried to reach the residential quarters, and the arrow slits of the round tower faced this area also.

Now, the whole exciting life of the castle had diminished and the town looked inwards upon itself to conduct a life of its own. It had its weekly market, and its town fairs, and was an agricultural centre with all the allied trades and crafts that go with farming. It was also a borough, and was described as such in one of its charters, so the burgesses had the right to hold a court, hear pleas, and levy fines. A bailiff presided over a court of trial and enquiry, which was an extension of the old manor court. Another officer was the reeve who collected fines and market tolls. An itinerant justice visited the town from time to time to inspect the records, and all must have been in order for Barnard Castle remained outside the direct control of the county sheriff until the reign of Henry VIII. The lord of the manor had a chief agent who resided in the town, probably in a large house towards the lower end of the Bank. The house outwardly now shows signs of seventeenth century architecture, but there is evidence of a much older structure and its traditional name is the Steward's House or the Manor House; it commanded a view of both the street and the Demesnes.

The street which is now called the Bank ran straight into Thorngate and down to the Tees, where there was a river crossing composed of stepping stones approached through thorn bushes. The whole street was known as Thorngate or Thorngate Bank. Among other buildings in that area was a friary with its own chapel and a quadrangle approached through an archway onto the main street. It was the house of the Augustinian friars who helped the spiritual and bodily welfare of the poor. Their land, which was given to them by the earl of Warwick, extended as far as the Demesnes and enclosed their own burial ground and kitchen garden.

Various lanes and alleyways connected Thorngate Bank with the Demesnes. One led directly to the mill (today's Gray Lane) and another, halfway up the street, was sufficiently important to be classed as one of the entries to the town, for it was (and is) called Broadgates. It was probably the route taken by cattle being driven to or from the Demesnes and the castle farm.

From the fourteenth century onwards there was another road into the town. It connected the main street to a bridge which crossed the Tees below the castle walls. The river had always acted as a natural moat, so when a bridge was built across it, the castle authorities built a sally port so that armed men could ride forth through the outer wall to defend the town end of the bridge against an attacking force advancing from the south bank. The bridge became known as the County Bridge because it linked the counties of Yorkshire and Durham. (This was the case until 1974 when the county boundaries were altered; both ends of the bridge are now in County Durham.) The bridge was a great improvement on the stepping stones which had hitherto been the only means of crossing the Tees into the southern part of the town, and it caused the creation of a new road, called Bridgegate.

The street of Newgate went in an easterly direction from the junction of Thorngate Bank and the Market Place, and contained St John's Hospital for Bedeswomen, founded by John Baliol. This establishment was to have a troubled history and as early as 1355 some people, now unknown, had misappropriated part of its revenue. Bishop Hatfield of Durham ordered them to be excommunicated with bell, book and candle.

The portions of land attached to houses in Newgate still extend to the Demesnes on one side and to the Back Lane on the other, suggesting that they are the relics of burgesses' plots granted by lords of the castle, and were an integral part of the town plan.

This arrangement of streets had the effect of placing the church at the centre of the town. Strictly speaking it was a chapel, for Barnard Castle was part of the parish of Gainford, but it was very important in the life of the town, not just as a place of worship but as a meeting place and a place of aesthetic pleasure. As the town grew in size, so did the church. In the thirteenth and fourteenth centuries, several additions were made to the original building: a south aisle was added and within it a chapel in which Robert de Mortham, Vicar of Gainford, was buried beneath his stone effigy. More windows were created and, in the second half of the fourteenth century, a tall leaden spire was raised on a short stone tower. The money for these developments presumably came from donations as well as regular income, but much of the capital probably came from St Mary's Abbey at York, for the first Bernard Baliol had put both the Gainford mother-church and the Barnard Castle church of St Mary into the possession of that abbey.

The church increased in grandeur as the castle declined in both appearance and significance, and the town's sense of independence grew still more. The feudal system was coming to an end, and throughout England there was an increasing awareness of what was much later referred to as 'the rights of man'. By the end of the fifteenth century almost all men were free from feudal duties to their lord, though they still had to attend the manor court two or three times a year to see how their town's affairs were being conducted.

Barnard Castle was, in fact, well to the fore in this new mood of freedom. For example, at the beginning of the fifteenth century a legal document was drawn up to nominate a new chaplain to serve in St Mary's Church, and it contains the significant phrase (in Latin) that 'the burgesses and the whole community of the town' were making the nomination. Another part of the document contains the expression 'the community or more influential part of the community' which shows that, though the

The common seal of the town's burgesses, attached to a document dated 1538.

town had a strong sense of unity, class distinctions were recognised within the community and that, of course, some men were more important than others. The document was sealed with the common seal of the town; 300 years earlier the seal of the Baliol family would have been used.

Barnard Castle was now a trading centre with improved communications because of the bridge over the Tees. In a national trend Teesdale had turned much of its arable land over to grazing, particularly for sheep, and the town had become a woollen centre, and had a large workforce of weavers and producers of knitted goods. Butchering flourished at the same time, and though the Town Moor, Town Fields and Town Pasture were still in common use, some arable land was fenced off and turned into pastures for sheep. More individual farmers had their own fields than ever before, and there were several wealthy families in the town.

Their influence was felt in various ways, including further gifts to St Mary's Church. One expensive gift was the massive font which still stands in the church. It is carved from so-called Tees marble, a form of limestone from the banks of the river about two miles (3km) below the town. The font bears the merchant's mark of the donor and two initials.

The greatest additions to the church in the fifteenth century came, however, from the traditional source, the generosity of the lord of the castle. Richard of Gloucester, later King Richard III, had acquired the title by his marriage to Anne, widow of Richard Neville, the earl of Warwick, whose family had received the lordship from Edward I. Richard took over the role of the Baliol family more than anyone else had done in the intervening period. His emblem, a silver boar, appears carved in stone in a window in the castle, and similar examples could once be seen in other parts of the town, suggesting his close relationship with the local community.

Of the three or four which remain, one boar is carved on a stone which forms part of an arch over the outside of the east window of the south transept of the church. It may be assumed, therefore, that this window and the widening of the south transept were the gifts of Richard. At the same approximate time the nave was heightened by the addition of a clerestory in the north and south walls, giving space and light to what may have been a rather gloomy building.

The chancel arch was also built at this time and ornamented with carvings of roses on a moulding which terminates at each side with a carved face — possibly one is a portrait of Richard as a tribute to his generosity. Over the arch, a filled-in doorway can still be seen, which gave access to a rood loft which seems to have been added at the same time.

In 1477 King Edward IV granted Richard a licence to found a choristers' college in Barnard Castle. There is no direct evidence that this was carried out, but it is likely that it was built, or at least started, in Newgate, for on a building near the church, on the opposite side of the street, was another carved boar. The building has been demolished and the boar is preserved in the Bowes Museum, but its original site would have been a suitable place for a choristers' college. If one of the heads on the chancel arch represents Richard, the other could represent Edward IV — but that is conjecture; some people consider one of the faces is female and may represent Richard's wife, Anne.

Another chapel in Newgate was attached to St John's Hospital, and it too benefited from patronage in the fifteenth century. Pope Alexander VI had heard of the devoted work of Christopher Hilton, the master of the hospital, and also learnt that the building was 'out of repair'. He therefore granted an indulgence to penitents who gave money for providing books, chalices, lamps, and 'ecclesiastic ornaments' for the chapel, and for repairing and maintaining the hospital. As the fifteenth century came to an end, John Baliol's hospital was struggling to survive, but the rest of the town which his family had founded was facing the future with confidence.

'This is a meatly praty town, having a good market, and meatly welle builded.' That was the opinion written in the notebook of the antiquary John Leyland (or Leland) when he visited Barnard Castle on his journey through England in the sixteenth century. Leyland approached Barnard Castle from the north-east, and as he rode along he noted rich farmland ('meately good corn and pasture') between Staindrop and Barnard Castle, which would partly account for the town's 'good market'. In referring to the 'well-built' town, Leyland would be assessing the stone-built houses which lined the eastern side of the Horse Market and the Market Place. Stone buildings impressed Leyland, and he noted with interest that Staindrop's church was built 'all of stone'. (So was St Mary's at Barnard Castle, though he did not mention it.) He liked the chapel inside the castle walls, considering it 'faire', and noticed a couple of tombs, one of them made of marble and both with effigies carved upon them. 'Sum say that they were of the Balliolles', he wrote cautiously; the inscription on the marble tombs was in French so the assertion was probably correct. He noted the spaciousness of the castle and its impressive residential quarters, and was very pleased with the wooded banks of the Tees.

Leyland crossed the river by the fourteenth century bridge which he referred to as 'the right fair Bridge on Tese of three arches'. There is no other source of information about the bridge at this time, so we must take his word for it that it once had three arches and was rebuilt, at a later date, with two. His journey downstream took him to the Egglestone Abbey church, less than two miles (3km) away, where he found two more tombs made of marble, and he realised where the material came from: 'Hard under the cliff by Egleston is found on each side of Tese very fair marble, wont to be taken up by the marbelers of Barnardes Castle and Egleston, and partly to have been wrought by them, and partly sold onwrought to others.'

There was a considerable trade in 'Tees Marble' in the district, and Leyland later reported seeing a quarry of 'black marble spotted with white' about a quarter of a mile (400m) from the abbey right beside the river. In the twentieth century a metal wedge was found tightly lodged in a crack between

'Tees Marble' which John Leyland noticed on the banks of the river near Egglestone Abbey.

two riverside rocks, a trace of a vanished industry from which was derived, among other things, the font in St Mary's Church.

Leyland gives a very favourable description of the town, suggesting that it was flourishing and impressive in appearance. His notes contain one memorable sentence which has often been quoted by more recent travellers: 'The Castelle of Barnard stondith stately upon Tese'. Despite its ruined condition it still does.

The town, with a flourishing market and a diversity of successful industries, demonstrated its prosperity in the dignified houses of its richer citizens. The lower end of the town seems to have been particularly popular with such people. Beside the entry to Broadgates stood the house now known as Blagrave's. The proportions and number of its rooms show it to have been a residence of some social standing; it had its own water supply in the vaulted cellars, in the form of a well that was thirty-six feet (11m) deep.

The Steward's House, farther down Thorngate Bank, and others in the area which now have an eighteenth century appearance, were already spacious residences in the sixteenth century. They were either detached houses, or much taller than their neighbours, for some of them had windows in the gable end which overlooked the river and the countryside beyond. On the eastern side of the street the large houses stood at the head of old burgesses' plots which extended to the Demesnes.

The comparatively new street of Bridgegate was also a pleasant residential area, at least on the side along which the river flowed, and there were also dignified houses in lower Thorngate. Dwellings in these streets are sometimes mentioned in wills that have survived from the sixteenth century. Cuthbert Hutchinson, for example, whose will was dated 1584, had a dwelling-house with garden in 'Briggate' and had 'Yeoman rights' to use the Demesnes, which shows his social status.

Some of these well-to-do men made benefactions to their poorer fellow townsmen, either in lump sums or in investments to continue into the future. In 1570 John Smayles left one sum of money to be put in the poor box and twice as much to be directly distributed to the poor, and in 1578 John Glenton 'devised certain lands' to provide an income for the use of the poor of the town. One of his fields was Glenton's Green beside Black Beck along the Harmire road, and Glenton's Charity survived into the twentieth century.

Such benefactions required local officers to oversee their proper distribution, and there were also collectors who could act at their discretion to encourage donations to help the poor. Officials could also build a poor house, but Barnard Castle's needy inhabitants waited until the second half of the seventeenth century before that provision was made for them.

Legislation had become necessary throughout the nation to deal with the problem of the poor. The plight of the needy had been made more desperate by King Henry VIII when he began to dissolve or disestablish monasteries and other religious foundations. Having received unfavourable reports on the conduct of such establishments, he sold their estates to local landowners and thus accumulated considerable wealth for his own use, a process which was completed by 1539. Part of the work of the monasteries had been to care for the poor so, when they were disestablished, local authority and private benevolence had to take over this aspect of their work.

There were various other ways in which Henry's actions had an effect on life in Barnard Castle. The Augustinian friary on Thorngate Bank was closed and demolished, and its stones were used in the walls of neighbouring houses. Other buildings were erected over the friary graveyard. The dissolution of the monasteries also led to changes in the organisation and funding of St Mary's Church, which had received financial help from St Mary's Abbey at York; it passed into the control of Trinity College, Cambridge, in whose hands the living still remains.

St John's Hospital in Newgate was included in the king's survey in 1536. Its income came not only from various parcels of land in the countryside around Barnard Castle, but also from Rievaulx Abbey which was disestablished soon afterwards. The report also disclosed that, once again, the hospital's affairs were being mismanaged and that money from other sources was either not being paid or someone else was receiving it. No mention was made of the hospital's share of income from the town's common fields, which had been part of John Baliol's original foundation.

This, too, had worsened the plight of the poor in the town, for the number of bedeswomen living in the building had fallen from thirteen to three. Any surplus income after paying for coal, food, and maintenance of the building went to the master of the hospital.

In 1535, after various edicts diminishing the Pope's influence in England, Henry VIII had proclaimed himself supreme head of the Church in his realm, and his decision, a year later, to seize St John's Hospital because some Roman Catholic rituals had been observed there shows the thoroughness with which he conducted his programme to establish a firm basis for the Church of England. The hospital itself was not abolished for it was a lay foundation, but from then on the master of the hospital was to be a Protestant appointed by the Lord Chancellor.

In 1545 Henry ordered another survey of Teesdale in which it was reported that the town had two schools, named as a grammar school and a song school. Perhaps the latter was the choristers' college founded by Richard III. Both schools were open to all Barnard Castle children and a priest was paid to conduct matins and evensong in the Anglican form of service.

These, on a national scale, were minor matters, though they must have caused controversy in the town, but within twenty-five years, in the reign of Elizabeth I, Barnard Castle found itself playing a crucial role in the religious debate that was still raging, either openly or secretly, throughout the country.

When Elizabeth I came to the throne in 1558, most of her subjects were able to remember when England was a Roman Catholic country. Now, by law, they were compelled to belong to the Church of England. Bitterness had been increased by the abolition of Latin in church services, and the issue of new prayer books led to uprisings and demonstrations in various parts of the country. Confusion had increased by the brief return of Roman Catholicism under Queen Mary, immediately before the accession of Elizabeth. Under the new queen, Anglicanism was firmly asserted again, with the Act of Supremacy giving all jurisdiction in ecclesiastical matters to the crown; the Act of Uniformity instituted fines for not attending church services; and in 1562 a law was passed excluding Catholics from Parliament.

Barnard Castle shared in the general unease, and then suddenly found itself having to play an important part, no matter how reluctantly, in national affairs. The earl of Westmorland, who owned Raby Castle, six miles (9.5km) away from Barnard Castle, began in partnership with the earl of Northumberland to organise armed resistance against the queen's reinforcement of 'the new religion' and aimed to replace her on the throne with Mary, Queen of Scots. Elizabeth knew of the earls' intentions and deprived them of some of their positions of authority; this increased their indignation and anger against the queen.

Another significant person who knew of the earls' intentions was Sir George Bowes (whose castle of Streatlam was only three miles (5km) from Barnard Castle); he was a staunch Protestant and resolved to oppose the earls. In the late summer of 1569 the earl of Northumberland met the earl of Westmorland with armed troops at Raby Castle, and Sir George Bowes wrote to the earl of Sussex, who commanded the queen's army in the North, telling him that much concern was being felt by loyal supporters of the queen.

Some inhabitants of Barnard Castle secretly sympathised with the rebellious earls, but others organised a watch to be kept on bridges and fords in case the earls brought an armed force to garrison the castle, which was at that time unoccupied. Sir George Bowes then took decisive action: he moved into the castle with his family to use it as a stronghold against the rebels, and he received promises from local supporters to join him there by nightfall on the same day.

Sir George was forty-two years old, and had military training and experience of Border warfare. There were two doubts in his mind: would he be joined by a sufficiently large force to man the sizeable castle, and, if so, would he be able to provide enough food and drink for them? The size of the rebel army was not known, but it was certain that Sir George's men would be outnumbered and his best hope would be to withstand a siege until the earl of Sussex marched to Barnard Castle from York where the queen's Army of the North was encamped. Sussex, however, also had too few men to meet the rebels in open battle; apart from foot soldiers he had only 400 horsemen, and they were not fully equipped. He needed reinforcements from the queen's Army of the South.

Despite the exchange of frequent letters, respectively asking for and promising speedy help, little progress was made. Within the castle, over 100 men of Barnard Castle had been joined by 200 foot soldiers and 100 horsemen 'of the gentry'. The local men were said to be 'well-appointed' with their own equipment.

Meanwhile the rebels were intimidating the neighbourhood with shows of force. Groups of men rode to and fro across the river, and Sir George Bowes was tempted to try to cut these groups off from one another, but the earl of Sussex advised caution. The rebels held Catholic services in Durham Cathedral and at Darlington. In Durham they broke communion tables and burned service books and committed other religious attrocities; at Darlington people were compelled by armed men to attend Mass. Emotions, including both wrath and fear, ran high. Sir George wrote 'at the Queen's Majesty's castle at Barnard Castle ... we have put ourselves in such readiness that, upon warning, we are all ready to serve Her Majesty with the bestowing of our lives'.

The people of the town were in a very agitated state of mind; there was no general consensus of opinion on attitude or action. Some joined the rebel forces; some were prepared to help in the defence of the castle; some stayed outwardly neutral and awaited the outcome of events. Some people actually ran away from the situation and hid in the woods and other rural retreats. Perhaps this category was most significant in showing the turmoil felt in people's minds, for it was late November, not the best time of year for living in a dense and neglected tract of hunting ground.

The numbers in the castle stayed constant, and a survey of arms showed that there were 104 spears, 85 bows, and 7 arquebusses (portable guns which could be mounted on tripods). The earl of Sussex wrote to the queen telling her that he hoped to raise over 1,000 men to help Sir George at 'Barney Castell'. The rebel army was by now a formidable force of between 1,000 and 1,500 horsemen, and possibly as many as 3,000 foot soldiers.

The rebels collected at Raby before heading south and — to almost everyone's surprise — they marched past Barnard Castle as if it was not there. They continued to advance and then, in another surprising move, suddenly retreated without having met with any opposition and marched towards Barnard Castle after all. Perhaps they feared the growing strength of the queen's army and felt the strategic need to have the use of a strong fortress, such as Barnard Castle, as their headquarters. At this decision some of their army became disenchanted and abandoned the cause, but thousands remained and they began to attack the castle, under the personal command of the earl of Westmorland, on the 3rd December 1569.

Sir George now had to face a siege, and the Army of the South was only as far north as Doncaster. The rebel forces were drawn up in battle formation where the defenders could see them, but Sir George's men were unable to fire effectively at them, for they had only three or four slings and one cast-iron cannon for long-range use.

The townspeople then had their first experience of warfare in their streets, for the rebels began to attack the outer wall of the castle on the section along the Horse Market and the Market Place. After three days the attacking force broke into the Town Ward, and the defenders fell back across an inner moat and continued the battle from the Middle Ward. Beyond that, across another moat, lay the Inner Ward in which Sir George and his family had their living quarters. It also contained the massive round tower, the last bulwark of defence.

Sir George on at least two occasions conducted sallies into the enemy camp, including a night attack in which he employed 200 men, but on one occasion two of his men were killed and thirty were captured by the earls' men, and during another nocturnal skirmish sixty-seven of his men were wounded by arquebus fire.

Much of the stress felt by a besieged army is psychological. The enemy is free to come and go, forage for food, and employ various tactics; the men in the castle are waiting for help, and provisions may be running low. There is a legend that the rebels taunted Sir George's men by chanting:

A coward, a coward o' Barney Castle
Daren't come out to fight a battle.

It would clearly have been imprudent if the loyalists had gone out to fight an open battle, but Sir George increasingly felt the threat of mutiny among his men within the castle. He and his family had been in the castle for a month and his men had been under siege for eleven days, food was running low and there was only water to drink (from wells within the castle) though Sir George sometimes issued it mixed with wine. Suddenly, in one disastrous day and night, surrender became inevitable. 226 of the beleaguered men leapt over the castle wall and joined the enemy. Thirty-five of them were killed or badly injured in the fall, breaking their necks or limbs. After a short while, 150 men who had continued to guard the gates against attack flung them open and joined the rebel force.

There was a sequel to their treachery for, on the same day, the wells of fresh water suddenly ran dry. There were two reservoirs on the edge of the Flatts, known as the Little Ever and the Larger Ever because they themselves never ran dry. They were probably the source of the water that supplied the wells in the castle, and the disloyal men had revealed the underground water-courses to the rebels, who had then diverted or dammed the flow. Nevertheless Sir George maintained that it was the desertions, rather than the loss of water, which led to his surrender on the 14th December 1569.

It must have been an unforgettable scene to those who stood in the Market Place to watch the loyal troop leave the castle. The earl of Westmorland was present at the surrender and allowed Sir George and his men to carry with them their personal armour and weapons, and he took no prisoners. This respectful conduct to an opponent, however, was not matched by events that then came to light: during the absence of the Bowes family, their own castle at Streatlam had been ransacked and looted.

However, Sir George felt he still had a job to do, so without delay he and his followers rode south to join the Queen's combined armies who by now were strong enough to face the rebel forces. Sir George was appointed provost marshall, and the Queen's army advanced through County Durham without any armed resistance. The earls' forces retreated with their cavalry, and their foot soldiers were disbanded. The Rising of the North, as the rebellion came to be called, ended with victory for the queen's men at a minor battle near Newcastle upon Tyne, and the leaders fled to Scotland and the Lake District. The earl of Northumberland died on the scaffold, still asserting the Pope's supremacy, and the earl of Westmorland lived abroad in relative obscurity until his death in 1601.

The turning point in the defeat of the rising had been the eleven days of siege at Barnard Castle. By holding up the rebels' advance, Sir George had provided a focal point for the whole campaign and had given time for the queen's armies to muster sufficient force eventually to dispel the rebels with ease. To make an example to all rebellious subjects the queen ordered that 700 of those involved in the rising should be executed. Sir George Bowes was put in charge of this, but it was not in his nature to be enthusiastic about it — so much so that he received letters from the earl of Sussex asking him not to be so dilatory over the retribution. The total of executions surely never reached the number which Elizabeth had demanded. In some villages no-one was executed, despite having had known rebels among their inhabitants. On the other hand, seven Staindrop men were executed, and sixteen out of eighty-three known rebels were hanged at Darlington. No-one from Barnard Castle was executed but it must have been a frightening time for many of the inhabitants.

Barnard Castle, both town and fortress, gained nothing from the important part it had played in quelling the Rising of the North. The castle had not been in good repair when Sir George had taken it over, and it had been further damaged in the siege, but no-one was appointed to see that it was repaired or maintained. Sir George Bowes himself did not fare much better; he received a gift of land as a reward from the queen, but the expense of defending Barnard Castle and of making good the looting and damage at Streatlam Castle was so great that he sold most of the queen's gift in an attempt to recoup his losses. He was never again a rich man.

He and succeeding members of the Bowes family maintained a kindly interest in the town. In 1579 he asked the head treasurer to allow him to fell sixty trees in Marwood Forest and Gainford Wood, some nine miles (14.5km) away, to be used in repairing the castle. Permission was refused. Sir George died in 1581 and in the same year the family repeated the request, which was again refused.

Ten years later Sir William Bowes, Sir George's eldest son, made an informative survey of the town, declaring that the terms of the Baliol charters were still being followed. The common pastures were still in use, and the inhabitants, despite the absence of a lord of the castle, were still legally bound to give two weeks' military service at one hour's notice if called to defend the Scottish borders. 400 men had turned out 'in the thirtieth year of the Queen's reign' (1587-8) to repel a reported

This carved stone is set in the northern approach wall of the County Bridge. It replaced an earlier one which bore the date 1569 (the year of the siege of the castle) not 1596.

foreign invasion at Hartlepool. Sir William said that Anglicanism was well-established in the town, the people being 'religious, of free will, yielding large maintenance to a preacher of the gospel'. It seems that there were 2,000 people living in the town at the end of the sixteenth century, of whom 240 were 'free-holders in good trade in reasonable state of wealth'. The weekly market was as prosperous at the end of the century as Leyland had found it to be fifty years earlier. Sir William Bowes called it 'a most plentiful market'.

It was fortunate for the town that this was so, for the castle was more and more showing signs of neglect. An inventory of the structure in 1592 showed that though the stone walls and lead roofs of the buildings were 'in reasonable good repair', there were windows without glass and doors without locks. Earlier reports had revealed that internal bridges, the gate house, and two of the towers were in need of repair. Perhaps, also, the outer wall had not been rebuilt at the point where the rebels had broken through in 1569.

The castle must have presented a sorry sight both to the residents of the town and the visitors who came in for the weekly market and the three annual fairs; the market streets ran parallel to the castle walls, still without houses on that side of the road, so it was impossible to ignore the contrast between the thriving inns, business premises and houses on the higher side of the street, and the dilapidated and deserted castle which stood just across the road from the market area. The building that had given birth, name and life to the town was effectively dead.

II

Self-help
1600–1800

Once again Barnard Castle had to prove its independence as a town, and this time the test was even more severe than in 1296 when the Baliols were banished. At that time the castle was still a suitable residence for successive lords of the manor who would keep an eye on the affairs of the town, but now, at the end of the sixteenth century, the castle was in no condition to accommodate an aristocratic administrator even if one had been appointed.

The damaged castle was never repaired, though the County Bridge which stood nearby was repaired and to some extent rebuilt in 1569. (A carved stone was inserted into its fabric with that date on it; unfortunately it was much later replaced by another stone on which the figures were transposed so that it now reads ' 1596'.)

A strengthened bridge and a weakened castle symbolised the condition of the town: it had a good system of communications for trade, but no castle to provide an administrative centre or to provide defence and protection. The town had lost its security.

Timely help, however, came from the king of England himself, James I. When, 300 years before, Edward I gave the lordship of Barnard Castle to the earl of Warwick and his successors, the king ensured the continuation of the market in the town, and in 1603 James I ensured the continuation of the existing fairs and markets by the issue of a royal charter. Since, however, there was now no resident lord of Barnard Castle, the king was emphatic that the terms of this charter should be maintained by self-government within the town itself. It was the duty of a court, known as the court leet, to see that the town's laws relating to markets and fairs were being obeyed, and to pass judgement on persons who were found guilty of infringing those rules. There was also a newly-formed committee, composed of fifteen men who were known as jurymen, which formulated new rules. These jurymen had to be freemen and were annually elected at a meeting of the town's burgesses, convened by the town steward who was directly answerable to the king.

Because Barnard Castle was an ancient borough, this committee was known as the Borough Court. There were also officials who had to carry out rules laid down by the old manor court, and to attend to orders made by the new Borough Court. The royal charter had expressed the duties of these officials in general terms and it was left to the Borough Court to specify what they had to do.

The most important of these officials was the constable, and he was at his busiest when the fairs took place. It was his task to regulate the conduct of visitors and the townspeople, and to deter them from fighting, or behaving in an unruly manner. On these occasions the town had to look at its best, and it was the constable's responsibility to see that the surface of the roads was in good condition and that the drainage ditches were clear. At all times the surface of the Market Place had to be in sound condition.

Throughout the year the constable's duties included the upkeep of the town lockup and the stocks, and the penning and feeding of stray animals which were to be kept in one of the town's two pinfolds or pounds until claimed by their owners. (One pound was at the foot of Galgate where the Methodist church now stands, and the other was in Newgate.) The constable had to supervise or remove vagrants who had entered the town, collect maintenance money from the fathers of illegitimate children, take care of waifs and strays, apprentice pauper children to useful trades, and to suppress riots and disperse unlawful assemblies.

To give dignity to the Borough Court and to give practical assistance to the constable in his sometimes dangerous duties, there was a town armoury, and another of the constable's tasks was to see that the weapons were kept in good condition and under close control. He kept them in his own house, except when he produced them for annual inspection by the court.

The court was keen on maintaining the town's sense of communal identity, and all inhabitants were required to know the boundaries of the common land which they were entitled to use, and strenuous efforts were made to ensure that cattle from the neighbouring countryside did not graze on Barnard Castle's own land. Such animals would be impounded and restored to their owners only on payment of a fine.

The court was also cautious about allowing into the town any 'strangers' who might lower the tone of Barnard Castle. It was impossible to keep a check on all people who visited the town on market days and fair days, because there were so many of them, but a law was made about lodgers or sub-tenants in houses in the town. Such persons had either to have been born in the town or, if they were 'strangers or foreigners', had to be registered each year.

A special court was established to deal with cases arising from disputes or bad behaviour involving visitors to fairs or markets. It was called a 'pie powder court', which was a corruption of the French expression *pied-poudreux*, meaning dusty-footed, referring to those who had travelled along the roads to reach Barnard Castle. On fair days and market days, the pie powder court took precedence over the ordinary Borough Court.

The great majority of laws which were passed by the Borough Court related to the people of Barnard Castle themselves. The rules came under three main headings: the conduct of the market; the general behaviour of the inhabitants; and safety precautions.

To see that goods sold at the market were of an acceptable standard, the Borough Court appointed officials called 'tasters'; their duties were to taste and test locally brewed ale, as well as meat, flour, and baked loaves. They also had to pay attention to the quality of lengths or pieces of tanned leather that were offered for sale, and specific mention was made of ready-made gloves and shoes. Barnard Castle enjoyed a high reputation for its leather goods and the court wanted to maintain it.

Some of the tasters' duties give an insight into unfair tricks which were practised by unscrupulous tradesmen. Oatmeal, for instance, had to be examined to see that it had not been adulterated with other substances and had not been dampened to increase its weight; the nap on cloth should not be artificially raised by using equipment intended for combing out wool, and lime was not to be used for bleaching cloth.

All goods sold on a market day had to be displayed in the public Market Place, not in back lanes or private houses, and no selling was to take place until the market bell had been rung.

The centre of the administration for the market was the tollbooth, a large building which stood in the Market Place. It was an outstanding feature of the main street, being about thirty yards (27m) long and consisting of two storeys with an outside staircase. The official weights and measures were kept in it, there was a cell in which disorderly people were kept while awaiting trial, and the town stocks stood against the wall facing the cobbled Market Place. It was from the tollbooth that the bell rang to signify the start of each market. The upper room was the meeting place of the Borough Court and, on appropriate days, of the pie powder court. Together with the church and the decaying castle, the tollbooth was one of the three dominant buildings of the town.

The laws which the court imposed on the townspeople themselves were based on the need for decent, considerate behaviour in a close-knit community. Townspeople were forbidden to allow infected animals to graze on common land, for example, and the people's common rights and duties had to be respected by everybody. The town owned one or two bulls for breeding purposes, and an order was issued that a town bull was not to be removed from the pasture between the 3rd May and 29th September; presumably the point was that selfish people might take the bull for use in their own private field when the people who were grazing cows on the common pasture were entitled to the bull's services.

The court was firm in its efforts to keep a peaceful relationship between members of the public, and it passed an order forbidding slander: fines were to be imposed on people who called anyone 'a thief, rogue, or villain' or uttered 'words of defamation' which they could not prove. If an argument came to blows resulting in bloodshed, or the drawing of swords even if no blood was shed, the constable had to arrest the culprit and not release him until he had paid a deposit to ensure that he kept the peace and had found a 'sufficient man' to answer for him if he repeated the offence.

The attitude of the seventeenth century's Borough Court echoed the sentiment of Hugh Baliol when, in the thirteenth century, he had hoped that the townspeople would accept his charter 'freely, quietly and wholly.' The health and safety regulations were also based on thoughtfulness and general common-sense. The risk of fire was a constant worry in a town with houses that had thatched roofs and a large amount of wood in their construction, so fire precautions were established. Household fires were allowed to smoulder even when not in use, partly because of the difficulty of relighting them in the days before matches. A 'piece of fire' from a neighbour's house was the easiest way of rekindling another person's fire, so a law was passed forbidding the carrying of fire in the street 'unless it was covered or otherwise sufficiently defended from the force of wind and from scattering'. It was also forbidden to store straw in places where a risk of fire might be expected.

In an age not always keen on maintaining standards of hygiene, it is interesting to note that one of the bylaws related to sewers. An open sewer ran from the Market Place, down a lane called Castle Wynd where the newer portion of the Kings Head (recently re-named the Charles Dickens) now stands, and flowed into the moat; it then ran down behind the houses on Thorngate Bank, and so into the River Tees. Every owner whose premises were adjacent to the sewer had to 'cleanse and scour' his section. To fulfil this rule a householder had to have a strong spirit of co-operation and community feeling, for in cleaning his own section he was dealing with the effluvia of people who lived uphill from him. No dung hills were allowed to stand in any street except Galgate, perhaps because it was so wide and rural in nature that it could accommodate 'nuisances' that would be intolerable in a more densely populated area.

The laws of which these are examples were passed over quite a long period of time and in an apparently random order, legislation being made as the need arose. There were some years in which a particularly large number of new rules came into operation; 1637, for example, was the year in which a determined effort was made to compel market traders to conform to proper standards.

Between the establishment of the Borough Court and 1637, there were three different owners of the castle. In 1615 King James I gave Barnard Castle to his eldest surviving son, the Prince of Wales, who took the financial benefits to help to maintain his own extravagant household. In 1625 James died, and the prince became King Charles I. The old king had not been financially secure and the new king was in real difficulties. A war against Spain had made it necessary to raise more money for national funds, and when Charles asked Parliament for help with his personal finances he was refused. What would have been a remote insignificant problem to the people of Barnard Castle suddenly loomed large when Charles began to review the property which he owned in various parts of the country. His dilapidated residence at Barnard Castle was of no great use to him and he began to look for a buyer.

He was successful in 1626 when he sold the castle to Sir Henry Vane, and over the next three years Sir Henry became the possessor of various other parcels of land including the Demesnes, the Flatts, and Marwood Chase together with the deer and other animals which it contained. Within ten years Sir Henry had acquired what was legally known as 'the Royal Borough of Barnard Castle and Raby'. In 1630 he decided to make Raby Castle his main residence, and began to dismantle Barnard Castle so that he could use its dressed stone and other useful materials to expand and strengthen Raby Castle. By 1633 his new home was in good enough condition to receive Charles I on his way to be crowned King of Scotland (as well as England), and the king visited Raby again in April 1639.

Though not residing in Barnard Castle, Sir Henry Vane did help the town in its efforts at self-government. He summoned an ancient institution called the Head Court to review the work that had been done by the Borough Court. The Head Court met in 1637 and in 1666, when old legislation was strengthened and confirmed, and new laws were inaugurated. Any shortcomings of the Borough Court, such as slackness that had crept in over guarding the common land from misuse, were rectified. In this case the jurymen of the borough were told to ride the boundaries on horseback, with as many of their fellow inhabitants as they chose to accompany them.

So it was good for the town that Sir Henry took this active interest in its affairs, but his dismantling of the castle was a different and more emotive matter. As the demolition men moved in and the horse-drawn wagons began to roll out of town, laden with the stones of the castle, the people were witnessing the destruction of what had once been the sole reason for the existence of their town. 'O, Misery!', wrote an anonymous author of a pamphlet published at the time. 'Can one hundred pounds worth of lead, iron, wood and stone be worth more than a castle which might have been a receptacle for a king and his whole train?'

While the castle was being diminished, other houses were being embellished. The house at the entry to Broadgates began to show more evidence of wealthy ownership. It became known as Blagrave's because that was the name of a seventeenth century owner, and on the first floor ceiling there is a decorative moulding with emblems of a rope and a rose, with the initials WIB signifying Joseph Blagrave and his wife. Improvements continued through the century, and an internal door is dated 1672.

Earlier the house had been an inn of some distinction, and there is a credible

Blagrave's House has had many uses in its long history.

tradition that it was here that Oliver Cromwell was accommodated when he visited the town in 1648. According to the diary of Christopher Sanderson Esq, Cromwell was conducted to his lodgings by various townspeople, and refreshed with mulled wine and short-cakes. Sanderson also records that the accession of James II was celebrated at Blagrave's, where he notes 'several gentle-men had a dinner and spent about twenty pounds; had two trumpeters, with silver trum-pets, and four drums; cost me 23 shillings.'

Lower down Thorngate Bank, the old Steward's House was by now a distinguished residence with ornamental stonework over the whole front-age. It was built in something like its present form in about 1621, the date which is carved on a fireplace in the house with the initials MS and AS representing a married couple. Two stewards in that century were Mark Shafto, and Sir James Shuttleworth who supervised the demolition of the castle on behalf of Sir Henry Vane.

The dismantling of the castle was completed by 1637, leaving a great amount of the building still standing, and it was not long before the townspeople began to take liberties with what remained. They began by gardening some of the land within the moat, for which two men were heavily fined in 1641. Undeterred by this, the townspeople began to erect buildings on that side of the street, using dressed stones from the castle walls. By 1655 the Borough Court seems to have accepted the practice, for it passed an order that simply forbade making a building or dumping rubbish 'that may do harm to the castle wall or the ground within the walls'. It was not long before several houses rose alongside the moat. It had become a waste space, except in its lower section where it was used as an open sewer, so in several places it was filled in and became an extension of the building plots. Even today, premises on that side of the Market Place and the Horse Market are built on land that slopes towards the castle wall and then levels out where the moat has been filled in.

The Golden Lion is an example. It is a three-storey inn bearing the date 1679. Behind its mock-Tudor front it is stone-built and the appearance of the stones suggests that they formerly were part of the castle wall. Behind the inn there is an outbuilding, made of similar stones, which according to oral tradition was once used as a butter market. It is quite likely that the town had such a building in the seventeenth century, for the Butter Market which now stands at the end of the Market Place was not built until 100 years later, and before that the open ground near the market would have been an ideal site, just across the road from the tollbooth where other perishable market goods were stored. The tollbooth was not only the legal and administrative

The Golden Lion was built with stones taken from the walls of the castle.

centre of the town, but also a market house. Meal and corn were stored there ready for sale, and meat was sold from the stalls which were kept in the tollbooth. Its full title was the 'tollbooth and shambles', an old word used at various times for a slaughter house or a place where raw meat was sold. Attached to the building was a blacksmith's forge for urgent repairs on market days or fair days.

Altogether, the tollbooth was a strange mixture of utilitarian and dignified functions; it was not always wholesome in odour or appearance, and to help it to achieve the impressiveness due to the Borough Court and to act as a reminder that jurymen still had to pay due regard to the lord of the manor, a stone carving of the arms of the Vane family was inserted into the wall of the upper storey. (Though still living in Raby Castle, Sir Henry Vane's grandson, Christopher, was created the first Lord Barnard in 1699.) Together with the size and position of the tollbooth itself, this ensured that both the townspeople and 'strangers' who attended the market were constantly reminded of the powers that ruled the town. Barnard Castle was an important agricultural centre, and in those days its Market Place was known as the Great Market.

The name distinguished it from the Horse Market which ran between the Great Market and lower Galgate, where the cattle market was held, thus creating a continuous market area of one fifth of a mile (300m). The law rigidly defining the area in which cattle could be sold was not passed until 1720, but such matters were generally accepted even before a law was passed, and the boundary stone of the cattle market was fixed at the widest part of Galgate.

Some bulls that were to be slaughtered for meat were taken into the area of the Great Market, for a bylaw passed in 1639 ordered that no butcher should kill a bull of two years old or more until it had been taken to the ring 'to be sufficiently baited', which was supposed to improve the flavour of the meat. The 'ring' was a metal circle of a few inches in diameter securely stapled into the ground; the bull was tethered to this by a length of rope about twenty feet (6m) long, and several dogs were encouraged to attack it. Sometimes the dogs were tossed by the bull's horns and sometimes they seized the bull in their teeth, often aiming for the muzzle. The bull was led away to be slaughtered after 'sufficient' baiting. In Barnard Castle the bull ring was outside the Raby Hotel, and it must have been a popular pastime, for the circular area just outside the reach of the bull was on one occasion the only surface in the market area which needed to be newly paved. No doubt dogs as well as their owners were excited by this violent sport, and there was a bylaw that no person should keep 'unreasonable' mongrel dogs or mastiffs unmuzzled in the streets.

Words like 'sufficiently' and 'unreasonable' suggest that the jurymen and the ordinary townsfolk had to use their discretion in maintaining the tone of their town. Self-government was working well, and led to a feeling of independence and confidence which pervaded the town.

The erection of houses, inns and business premises along the western edge of the market areas was the most significant ingredient in this new mood. As these buildings rose, the castle disappeared from view. Once, it had dominated the town centre; now, in the seventeenth century, the town's businessmen and householders looked across the street at each other's premises, not at the residence of their overlord. The result of this was not just a closed street scene; it symbolised and helped to create a strong community spirit.

Some events in seventeenth century Barnard Castle were, however, beyond the control of local government. One was the succession of epidemics of fatal infectious

The buildings on the right-hand side of the market streets stand on what was once an open slope running down to the castle moat.

diseases which surged through Teesdale from time to time. In 1636 'the plague' struck at Winston and at nearby Osmondcroft, some six miles (9.5km) from Barnard Castle, so virulently that the July fair in the town had to be cancelled; in 1644 it badly afflicted the Romaldkirk area, six miles (9.5km) away in the opposite direction, and in 1645 an outbreak of the illness 'made great havoc' in Barnard Castle itself, according to Christopher Sanderson's diary.

Teesdale suffered again in 1663 and 1665 (the year of the Great Plague which struck London) and, as a precaution, trade was sometimes conducted far away from buildings which might be contaminated. One example of a temporary trading place was the Butter Stone, standing in open moorland overlooking the village of Cotherstone, four miles (6.5km) from Barnard Castle. Vendors placed their goods on or beside the large stone and then retreated to a safe distance, whilst a purchaser left his money in a bowl of vinegar on the stone. He then went home with his purchase and the vendor removed the money. If the object of the sale was an animal, it was tethered near the stone. A road from Barnard Castle to Baldersdale, the next valley, crossed a road to Cotherstone within forty yards (36m) of the Butter Stone, making it a convenient place for open-air trading in dangerous times.

Though such matters were tragic and serious disruptions to the town's well-being and economy, a more constant financial worry was the plight of the town's poorest inhabitants. A poor rate was levied on more prosperous people and administered by

An unpretentious cottage stands beside a grander three-storeyed house in old Bridgegate. Each has a passageway leading to buildings in yards running between the road and the river. *(From an original watercolour by Lucy Errington.)*

elected honorary officials who had to use their discretion in distributing the funds. This was a task which earned them much criticism from those who paid to the poor rate and who complained that some paupers could find work but would not try, and that others 'belonged' to another parish and should receive poor relief from their own ratepayers.

In 1662 an act called the Law of Settlement stated that a 'stranger' with no prospect of work within forty days could be sent back to his native parish. On the other hand, a pauper who had worked for forty days in a parish could claim relief from his 'adopted' parish. It was all very undignified and led to numerous legal wrangles.

All Barnard Castle's paupers were on 'outside relief', for the town had no poor house. Many people thought that administration would be helped if some of the paupers lived in an institution under the control and help of a master of the poor house. Money was left for the purpose in benefactors' wills; others gave buildings which could be leased to provide a regular income. Towards the end of the seventeenth century a poor house was built on a plot of land in Thorngate, facing onto the Demesnes, with a long vegetable garden in which the inhabitants could work if they were able.

Since Barnard Castle was a market town set in a spacious countryside, the prospect of 'able' paupers finding work varied seasonally: haytime and harvest needed more workers than seed-time and ploughing. The town was crowded at fair-times and market days, and quiet at other times, so casual labour tended to be irregular.

The most flourishing industry in the town itself was based on leather. Barnard Castle's tanning process and its leather goods were highly regarded over a wide area. There were four sets of tan-pits in the town in which skins were soaked for a year, after being stamped with the date on which treatment was begun, and part of the inspectors' (or testers') duties was to check on this procedure, and their care was rewarded by the town's great reputation for leather.

Ralph Thoresby, a visitor to Barnard Castle in 1694, noted that leather was the main industry of the town, 'now chiefly famous for bridles there made'. Lady Ann Clifford, countess of Appleby Castle, noted in her housekeeping account book that she had sent one of her men over the Pennines to buy harness for her at Barnard Castle.

Unhappily, this excellent trade was suddenly brought to the brink of disaster. In an effort to curb Britain's national debt, Parliament gathered taxes by a wide variety of methods, one of which was to impose a tax on leather. This had a devastating effect on the town's industry and in 1698 the leather workers petitioned Parliament, as recorded in the journal of the House of Commons:

> A petition of the tanners, leather dressers, and glovers of the town of Barnard Castle in the County of Durham was presented to the House and read, setting forth, that the petitioners, living at a great distance from London, and other trading towns, their returns are so small that they can scarce maintain their families; and since the duty upon leather, their trades are very much decayed, and their families reduced to the utmost extremity; and praying upon the House to raise money, other than by a tax upon leather.

Parliament decided 'that the said petition do lie upon the table' or, in other words, that nothing be done at present; it 'lay on the table' for well over 100 years till the tax on leather was halved in 1822 and abolished in 1830.

Meanwhile, in 1707, a law passed by the Borough Court read: 'whereas the town of Barnard Castle hath been anciently reputed for tanning of good leather, and for preservation of the same; ordered, that no tanner sell, stall, or expose hides not sufficiently tanned and dressed.' This suggests that the town's reputation was suffering because some tanners had been producing inferior leathers in order to achieve a quick turn-over to compensate for their losses incurred by the tax.

Despite taxation, tanning survived, and even had a considerable revival in the eighteenth century, but was eventually overtaken by the woollen industry, after a hundred years of rivalry. The trades continued simultaneously, and in 1720 the two main products of the town were woollen stockings and leather bridles.

It was in the 1720s that Daniel Defoe, the author of *Robinson Crusoe*, travelled to Barnard Castle via North Yorkshire, and noted that 'the manufacture of yarn stockings continues thus far but not much farther.' The woollen workers produced knitted garments and lengths of woven worsted cloth, but by about 1760 the worsted industry had declined in the face of increased competition. The local manufacturers then tried to undercut their rivals in other towns by producing cheaper cloth, but the inferior product lost them more custom, and workers became unemployed, some looking elsewhere for work. One rival town was Darlington, which had been the same size as Barnard Castle earlier in the century, but by 1792 Darlington had a population of 5,190 while Barnard Castle's was only 2,920.

Leather revived in 1777 when a successful new firm was founded by Anthony and Richard Steele with premises in Bridgegate and, later, Newgate. They imported hides from India and sold their wares over a wide area of Britain, travelling on horseback far into Scotland delivering their products and seeking new orders. High-class shoes made from a glossy leather called cordova were one of the firm's specialities, as well as work clogs and everyday shoes.

An engraving showing men fishing with a net attached to a boat on still water near Ullathornes Mill.

The Butter Market, commonly known as the Market Cross; immediately to its right (partly obscured) is the house of Thomas Breaks, who gave the Butter Market to the town.

However, dyed woollen goods again became the town's most successful industry in the eighteenth century. The water of the River Tees was found to be an excellent medium for dyes and Barnard Castle became notable for its production of 'tammy', a colourful cloth produced in thirty-yard (27.5m) lengths and popular in Scotland. By the 1790s an estimated 400 weavers worked in the town out of a total population of 3,000. They worked not only in the riverside mills in Bridgegate, but also in upper storeys of their homes where rows of windows, separated only by stone mullions, allowed as much light as possible to fall on the looms. Some of these houses can still be seen in Thorngate.

Just outside the town's boundary, on the Yorkshire bank of the river, was a large flax factory which drew most of its workforce from Barnard Castle. This mill, Ullathornes, started in 1760 and grew in size until it enjoyed a worldwide market, exporting shoe-thread to Spain, Turkey and the British colonies, and supplying goods to French shoemakers and saddlers. Other products included rope and twine which were used for a wide variety of purposes including nets for salmon fishing. Ullathornes and another mill at the end of Thorngate began as water mills, each directing the flow of the Tees towards the mill race by a weir. The weirs raised the level of the Tees and caused it to run more smoothly, with the result that small boats could be used by fishermen.

It was possible to catch salmon just outside the factory which had made the net being used to entrap the fish; the river may have been discoloured by the dyes, but since they were made from vegetable and other natural substances they did no harm to the fish. Ullathornes also owned a flax mill on the Durham side of the Tees, a third of a mile (530m) downstream from the Demesnes corn mill.

There were also flax mills at Darlington, and it was a Darlington man and a Barnard Castle man who, working together, invented the first mechanical means of spinning flax. They were John Kendrew and Thomas Porthouse, financed by Backhouses, the banking family of Darlington. The machine was patented in 1787 and could do the work of four persons. It did not, however, have the impact on local employment which might have been expected. Women who did the spinning were so poorly paid that the mill-owners found it more economical to continue to employ them rather than to spend money on new machinery.

Meanwhile Barnard Castle's traditional role of market centre continued in the upper part of the town, where the market area was officially divided into various specific areas for different purposes, including sub-divisions of the Great Market for 'corn, grain and roots'. The Horse Market was also important at this time. On his journey through Britain, Daniel Defoe was enthusiastic about the horses which he saw between Bedale and Durham, saying that 'they would outdo for speed and strength the swiftest horse that was ever bred in Turkey or Barbary'. As he approached Barnard Castle he noticed that horse breeders and dealers increased in number, and reported: 'Here we saw some very fine horses indeed'. He added that they were expensive but justified the high prices that were asked for them.

Barnard Castle was a prosperous place in the eighteenth century, and it had an extensive system of transport for despatching the goods which it produced. It had three firms of carriers who sent wagons once a week to Darlington and Newcastle on Thursdays, and to Richmond in Yorkshire on Saturdays. Another went to Stockton on Thursdays and returned the following day, thus giving access to and from sea-going vessels at the busy Teesside port. Three wagons each week linked Barnard Castle with London, and passengers and parcels could travel on stage-coaches to and from the capital by using local transport to join or leave the coaches at Darlington or Greta Bridge. These stage-coaches travelled daily, but the journey between London and Barnard Castle took thirty hours. Passengers who could afford to do so were well advised to make at least one overnight stop on the journey, but it was not strictly necessary as the coaches kept going throughout the night.

Many of the buildings which still stand in Barnard Castle bear witness to the town's prosperity in the eighteenth century. There was a curving row of fine dignified houses on the higher side of the Market Place and occasional examples along the same side of the Horse Market, replacing a succession of older houses that had stood on those sites since medieval days. Apart from those two streets, it was Bridgegate which was the most densely built-up area, and it unfortunately lacked the healthy situation of the streets that stood higher up the town.

Bridgegate's narrow curving road was lined with houses interspersed here and there with industrial buildings. Some of the large houses were dignified three-storeyed residences, and others were unpretentious cottages. The houses were built in a continuous row and, in the absence of gaps between them, they had archways which led to outbuildings and dwellings in enclosed yards behind the houses. These were airless, particularly on the north side of the street where the yards terminated at the cliff on which the castle stood. Some of the smaller houses were even built on the upper part of the cliff itself, with the natural rock or the castle wall forming the back wall of the houses.

There was so little space in Bridgegate that some of the workers' houses were built high on the cliff, using part of the castle itself as their rear walls.

Two large houses were linked together to enlarge the original residence of Sir John Hullock, on the left of the pair.

Thorngate and the Bank also contained many dignified houses alternating with workers' homes. Thorngate showed the biggest social contrast in Barnard Castle, where the poor house stood only a few yards away from the richest and grandest house in the town. This house, later known as Thorngate House, was the home of Sir John Hullock, an eminent lawyer who became a baron of the Exchequer and a circuit judge. He enlarged his already spacious house by linking it with its neighbour. In this fine town-house he entertained visiting judges who were presiding over courts in the North-East.

These large buildings provided a contrast to earlier houses by being roofed with stone slabs from local quarries, though the traditional thatch was still common throughout the town. While the new style of housing was established in the main streets, Galgate still preserved its rural atmosphere. Its houses were much more widely spaced, with fields and gardens between them, though a few 'town houses' began to appear. One of them was a charming long building of 1760 which was called the Grove and was the home of William Hutchinson, author of a notable history of County Durham. He planted trees in his grounds which extended to the Back Lane, which in turn bounded the old Town Fields.

Galgate itself was planted with two clumps of trees, one at the top of the street where public hangings had once taken place, and the other crowning the slope where Marshall Street stands today. A writer early in the nineteenth century said that Galgate looked like a road leading to a village.

The dignity of the town centre was enhanced in 1774 by the addition of a new Butter Market, the gift of Thomas Breaks who lived nearby, at the top of the Bank. Its function was to provide shelter for the farmers' wives who sold dairy produce each Wednesday. The Butter Market, which has since been called both the Town Hall and, more recently, the Market Cross, stood in a prominent position at the very heart of the town at the junction of three roads, the Market Place, Thorngate Bank, and Newgate.

The street of Newgate grew in importance after the construction of the Abbey Bridge in 1773; this crossed the Tees about two miles (3km) below the town, and its new significance as an eastern approach can be judged by the fact that early in the next century the post office was moved from Bridgegate to Newgate.

At the same time as the Butter Market was being built, the church spire was demolished; it had lasted from medieval times but had eventually become unsafe. To compensate for this loss of height, the church tower on which the spire had been mounted was raised to sixty feet (18m) and was surmounted by a small square towerlet with a pointed roof. The old spire can be seen on the first known picture of Barnard Castle, engraved by Samuel and Nathaniel Buck and published in 1728. Its main subject is the ruined castle, but it also shows a few details of the town including the little building on the County Bridge, which has been conjectured to have been a chapel but was certainly used as a house later in the century. The castle was increasingly subject to natural decay, and towards the end of the century part of the wall fell over the cliff beyond the western end of Bridgegate, but still nothing was done to preserve it.

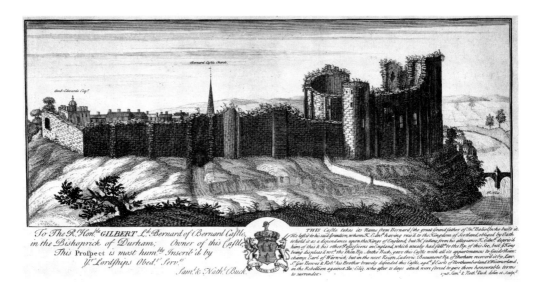

The castle and some elements of the town, engraved by Samuel and Nathaniel Buck in 1728.

Considerable attention was, however, given to repairing the surface of the streets in the town, which had become very unsatisfactory indeed. The surveyors' report for 1767 includes details such as: 'The street of Newgate is needful of immediate repairs and the sides of the street are so ruinous as to be very dangerous for foot passengers in the night.' The street of Bridgegate was so ruinous that it was 'dangerous for passengers on horseback and carriages'. Gutters ran down the side of some streets so that rainwater could run away and carry some rubbish with it. Houses on the east side of Galgate were reached by flat stones which were laid over this little ditch or stream, but debris was wedged under some of them and the stream flowed onto the road. Bits of timber, loose stones and dung also littered the road.

Some of the difficulties could be overcome simply by removing the rubbish, but in other places, surfaces were repaired with stone and gravel, and paving slabs. Stone was quarried from the sloping fields above the Westwick road and was stacked, ready for use, at the east end of Newgate. Other stones (or cobbles) could be taken from rivers and streams. To help to maintain the surface of Galgate, the old Back Lane was used as a town 'ring road' for heavy vehicles; in one instance, a coal-cart pulled by three horses came down Galgate and the driver was reported to the authorities. The footpath up the side of Thorngate Bank was made into steps to enable pedestrians to walk up it more easily.

Four surveyors supervised (without payment) the work of repair and maintenance which was performed by able-bodied householders or tenants, who each gave an agreed number of days of 'statute labour' each year. As an alternative they could pay someone else to do the work for them, and richer householders had to provide a cart with horses or oxen. Men under eighteen years old or over sixty-five were exempt from any service, as were apprentices to a craft or trade. Of the 700 people approached between the autumns of 1767 and 1768, only a dozen culpably failed to give help, though many others were excused on grounds of age or infirmity.

Over the twelve months, forty-eight householders had moved to some other town or village, or were said to be 'travelling' or employed at a distance. Allowing that some had taken their families with them, the total of people who had moved away from Barnard Castle in one year was perhaps nearly 200. In most cases their destinations were known; it was a period of decline in the town's textile trade and over twenty of the 'missing' men had gone to other textile centres.

The scheme for repairing roads and footpaths was executed in a piecemeal way, as the problems varied from street to street, but it was another notable attempt at self-help, if only partly successful. Though the town had various schemes and owned equipment for regulating several aspects of its life, it still had no fire engine and had to rely on the equipment and brigades belonging to insurance companies, the nearest of which was at Darlington, sixteen miles (25km) away.

In 1747 a big fire destroyed several houses in Barnard Castle, and in the following year another fire began in Robert Newby's barber's shop, and destroyed his premises and two of his neighbours' buildings before it was extinguished with the help of the lord of the manor's own fire engine from Raby. Later his lordship made a gift of it to the town and it was, after some protracted arguments, kept in St Mary's Church near the north door.

It was a great asset to the town, but it became involved in a contentious situation when John Wesley, the founder of Methodism, paid his first visit to Barnard Castle in 1752. He began to address a crowd which had gathered at the junction of the Horse Market and the Market Place but, according to his journal, his supporters were prevented from hearing properly by an unruly section of the crowd who brought out the town's fire engine in order to soak the devoted listeners. Another account suggests that the target for the stream of water was Wesley himself, but one of his supporters seized the hose and directed it at the crowd instead.

John Wesley was not the first man to bring Methodism to Barnard Castle, for he was preceded by Joseph Cheesebrough, a native of the town, who had learnt of the

The Wesleyan chapel was built in 1764 over the narrow thoroughfare called Broadgates. On the left is the minister's house which was added in 1798. *(From Anthony Steele's* History of Methodism in Barnard Castle and the principal places in the Dales Circuit, *1857.)*

Methodist movement in Leeds, and William Darney, who preached in Barnard Castle and upper Teesdale, but Wesley visited the town almost twenty times. He preached on the Demesnes and other open areas, for there was no Methodist chapel in Barnard Castle until 1765. There was a meeting house, however, available to various religious bodies, in the building which stands over the footpath known as the Hole in the Wall, between Newgate and the Back Lane, and he also preached there.

Wesley records a great improvement in the behaviour of local people at religious meetings. 'Are these the people', he wrote in 1761, 'who a few years ago were like roaring lions? They are now as quiet as lambs.' He called them 'simple, loving, earnest people'. By 1764 work was well in hand to create a chapel for the new Society of Methodists. It was to stand at the eastern end of Broadgates, near the top of the Demesnes. Stone was quarried from land nearby, and to a considerable extent the chapel was literally built by the members themselves; after their ordinary day's work the men worked on the stone while the women carried water to mix with the lime. Their work continued in the face of fierce opposition. Two successive curates-in-charge of St Mary's Anglican Church openly spoke against Methodism and sometimes parts of the newly-built walls of the Broadgates Chapel were pulled down during the night by the enemies of Wesleyanism. But it was finished eventually, with a tunnel on the ground floor to accommodate the ancient route between the Bank and the Demesnes, and the inaugural sermon was preached by John Wesley himself on the 13th April 1765.

On several occasions Wesley's congregations included members of the militia, for the town had become a military centre for the first time since 1569. The lord of the manor, who in 1754 acquired the title of Viscount Barnard and earl of Darlington, was asked to raise a body of militia in 1758. He chose to base it at Barnard Castle, the nearest town to his castle at Raby. The Durham Militia, as it was called, consisted of 365 men under the command of officers who had to be persons of some wealth and social standing. The militia received twenty-eight days of training each year and could be called up for full-time service in national emergency. Summer camps were animated occasions in Barnard Castle as, apart from the serious training, there was a holiday atmosphere and some element of irresponsibility when the part-time soldiers mingled with the local inhabitants. The militia brought colour and music to the town, and there was sometimes dancing in the streets.

The soldiers also brought a temporary boost to trade, which was particularly welcome to the proprietors of the numerous public houses who depended on market days for much of their profits throughout the year. Some of them provided entertainments for additional income: there was cock-fighting at the Red Lion, for example. There was also a cock-pit on the east side of the Bank, up the Wycliffe Yard, where large sums of money changed hands in the form of wagers on busy days.

Extra crowds continued to swell the streets on fair days and hirings days when, on Martinmas Day (17th November), farmworkers came into town to find work with a different master if they wanted a change or if their service had been terminated. Farmers ran their eyes over the assembled workers to choose new employees, and when the anxious day was over entertainments eased the tension. In 1791 there was a dancing bear and various side shows, and theatrical performances at the Queens Head, near the corner of Newgate and the Market Place.

Apart from its agricultural and industrial aspects, Barnard Castle had become quite a 'society' town, too. A retired general, an eminent lawyer, four surgeons, a few physicians, some solicitors, and the officers of the militia all created, with their wives and families, a social sphere of their own. Evening parties were frequent, despite difficulties on winter evenings; the streets were lit by oil-lamps which were sometimes extinguished by the wind or naughty boys, and the footpaths were in a dreadful state despite the efforts of the surveyors. Still, as Dr George Edwards, a well-to-do local physician, said, 'even ladies' found their way to and from their hosts' and hostesses' houses.

Dr Edwards was a benevolent man who felt that the town's streets could be much improved if all the inhabitants were more co-operative. As it was, posts and fences jutted out onto the pavements and people committed insanitary 'nuisances' beside them; the road opposite the thatched cottages in upper Galgate was disfigured with dung heaps, pig sties, hayricks and loose stones. Carts stood about at random, and all sorts of rubbish lay in lower Galgate and the Horse Market, where inhabitants had lazily thrown it despite the provision of a large rubbish tip beside the castle, in the ravine which ran from the bottom of Galgate towards the river.

Rubbish in the streets was one of the problems facing a parochial organisation known as the Vestry, which had taken over the administration of such matters as poor relief and, in 1806, the repair of highways. Barnard Castle was still part of the parish of Gainford, but as a 'township' it was entitled to this parochial form of local government, with the power to levy a rate for funding its duties. In the eighteenth century the township had an Open Vestry, which meant that any male ratepayer had a right to vote on any proposal, though not many people took advantage of their right; in 1814 the Vestry minute book records a meeting attended by the curate-in-charge, the chapel wardens and the 'principle inhabitants of the townsfolk of Barnard Castle'. Little seems to have changed in that way since 1401 when a document referred to 'the more influential part of the community of Barnard Castle'. In 1819 the Open

Vestry was replaced by a Select Vestry consisting of a committee with executive powers, but the same persons' names appear in the minute book despite the change of system.

When the Vestry appointed a scavenger to clear the streets, and set about re-paving the footpaths and providing pedestrian crossings, and levelling out bumps and hollows in the road, the scheme was so expensive that a public subscription fund was opened. The expense of having a scavenger was to be defrayed by selling the manure which he collected from the streets.

As in all ages, there were people who disregarded both civil and ecclesiastical authority. One such person was Cuthbert Hilton, who conducted illicit weddings on the middle of the County Bridge which crossed the common boundary of the two bishoprics of Durham and of Chester. A so-called marriage service which was conducted exactly on the boundary might be considered to be outside the jurisdiction of either of the bishops. Hilton conducted the ceremony on this principle and, if the tradition is true, he instructed the bride and groom to jump over a broom-shank so that they were briefly in mid-air while he rapidly pronounced them man and wife. In some northern parts of the country the expression living 'over the brush' is still used for unmarried couples living together.

Cuthbert Hilton was not the only local man to have performed such ceremonies. Over 100 years earlier a man conducted secret 'weddings' in Bridgegate and in 1716, when there were reports of an alleged marriage between an itinerant tinker and a twelve year old girl, enquiries revealed that similar ceremonies had taken place at Whorlton, four miles (6.5km) downstream.

The River Tees played an important part in the life of Barnard Castle: it was important to industry, and it provided salmon and trout for sport and food, and in severe winters it brought both entertainment and danger. Though it is in general a fast-flowing river, the Tees has long stretches of smooth water, and the three weirs near Barnard Castle increased the number of areas that could be used for skating. In 1740 horse races were held on the ice, and drinks were sold in tents on the frozen pool beside the County Bridge, with the customers and onlookers being warmed by fires burning in braziers standing on the ice.

Danger came when the thaw started. In 1780, after an eight-week frost, the thaw caused floods that broke up parts of the mill weirs, and in 1784 three boys who had been playing on the ice were swept away on floes that were six inches (15cm) thick. The boys were rescued at the flax mill, called Low Mill, downstream of the town on the Durham side of the river.

The chief danger, however, was the floods to which Defoe was referring when he wrote: 'The Tees is a terrible river, so rapid'. There was one particularly sudden kind of flood called the 'Roll' in which a wall of water swept down Teesdale at great speed. This happened when a quick thaw or heavy rainfall, or both, occurred in the upper dale, when flooded tributaries from adjoining valleys augmented the swollen waters of the Tees. Before reservoirs were built in the upper Tees and the tributary valleys, the Roll was a recurrent feature of life in Barnard Castle. Parents warned children of the dangers of playing near the river by inventing a mythical water-witch named Peg Powler who would seize unwary children and drag them below the water. The flakes of foam swirling on the surface of the rising Tees were referred to as the soap-suds from Peg Powler's wash-tub which she had emptied into the river. Sometimes the river rose rapidly over several minutes rather than increasing with a sudden rush of water; in either case observers sometimes felt an eerie stillness in the air which gave rise to fears of the flood that was to come.

A watercolour by Thomas Hearne (1744-1817).

The greatest flood came in 1771. The autumn of that year was very wet and November was especially so. On Thursday the 14th, the level of the Tees was very high and still rising, and on the following day people living at Bridge End (on the south bank) and in Thorngate and Bridgegate were carrying armfuls of clothing and were pushing hand-carts of furniture as they sought temporary accommodation away from the river. The river rose to, as far as was known, an unprecedented level. Half a mile (0.8km) above the town it broke through a riverside quarry, leased by a man called Waterman on the Yorkshire side of the river, and deposited a large piece of the riverbank into the middle of the Tees, where it is still known to some people as Watermans Island.

At Barnard Castle the river rose above the arch on the Yorkshire side of the stone bridge, and the pent-up water broke through the parapet and surged down the slope of the bridge, into the road, and struck with appalling force the houses of Bridge End. Eight of them were demolished instantly. The road surface and the topsoil at that end of the bridge were washed away, exposing the solid rock twelve feet (3.5m) below. Until the approach road to the bridge was restored, only pedestrians could use the bridge and they had to climb a ladder to do so. Reports say that houses were also destroyed in Bridgegate and riverside mills were inundated, with damage to their contents and machinery. Some people were marooned overnight in the upper storeys of their houses and listened to the destruction continuing around them in the darkness.

One man who was a weaver who dyed his own goods had a curious experience. He abandoned some materials in his dye-kettle in the basement of his house, and after the flood had subsided he returned to examine his goods, expecting to find them ruined. Having cleared away sand and mud from the dye-kettle, he was astonished to find that his cloth had acquired an unusually good quality of colour. London buyers to whom he sent the goods urged him to supply them with more but, as an old account expresses it, the dyer 'not being again assisted by the genius of the river, failed in every attempt to do it'.

The small building which stood on the centre of the bridge seems to have survived the flood. At the time it was the home of a cobbler who evacuated his little house as the river rose. Two watercolours by Thomas Hearne show the house on the bridge in 1778, and J M W Turner on his northern tour of 1816 also recorded it as still standing. An engraving published in 1823 shows no house on the bridge, however, so it must have been demolished between 1816 and 1823. Whatever condition it was left in after the flood, the house must have lost some of its attraction as a picturesque residence overlooking the Tees.

The south arch of the County Bridge and, beside it, the house of the weaver whose dye-kettle was inundated during the great flood of 1771.

III

Dark Days
1800–1850

Though the River Tees was both useful and, at times, dangerous, its chief merit lay in providing Barnard Castle with a beautiful environment. The town's streets sloped down to its banks, flanked on the east by the green slopes of the Town Fields and the Demesnes, and on the west by Flatts Woods, through which a tributary (first called Woolhouse Beck, and then Percy Beck) flowed into the Tees. The river itself curved gracefully round the lower end of the town, so that half the town was bordered by running water.

In 1794 William Hutchinson, the historian, wrote:

'The town of Castle Barnard is situated on the Southern inclination of a hill descending swiftly to the River Tees. The environs of this place are remarkably beautiful, and the vale of Tees everywhere abounds with the noblest and most romantic landscapes.'

Everyone in the town must have been aware of its rural surroundings, for Barnard Castle still consisted of one long main street joined at right-angles by only two other

'The town of Castle Barnard is situated … on a hill descending swiftly to the River Tees.'

streets, Newgate and Bridgegate. Even the crowded areas of the town were linked to the countryside by alleyways and yards which ran from Thorngate and the Bank onto the Demesnes which, as Mr Hutchinson reported, were 'let out in pasturage' and were 'constantly open to the inhabitants for exercise and pleasure'. Footpaths ran along the riverside as far as the Abbey Bridge (which was known as 'Newbridge' for a few decades after it was built) and paths extended from the west end of Bridgegate, along the wooded areas beside the Tees and through parts of Flatts Woods. These woods had no footbridges over the stream, and the paths and fords had simply come into existence as the easiest routes between the town and the neighbouring countryside.

Dr George Edwards, however, saw the woods as an area in which his fellow townsmen could enjoy healthy exercise in beautiful surroundings, so, at his own expense and with the permission of the earl of Darlington who owned the woods, he constructed additional paths which led into parts that had not hitherto been open to the public. The paths, with only a few modifications, are still in use and much enjoyed today.

The doctor also pointed out a mineral spring whose waters could be drunk by residents and visitors. He cautiously said that he thought the spring was probably health-giving and added, with more certainty, 'Its valuable laxative quality has, I know, been ascertained'. One mineral spring emerged beside the Tees two miles (3km) above the town, another two came out near the Castle Scar, and another, the Red Well, was near Harmire Road on the Town Moor. It could be reached along the road or by walking along one of the new paths in Flatts Woods and crossing the road. The Red Well was named from the colour of the stain left on the stone over which the mineral spring flowed, and its importance was suggested by the fact that the footpath extended only as far as the Red Well itself, and that a public house standing by Harmire Road later took its name from the mineral spring.

The ancient Town Moor in which the Red Well was situated was, however, in a neglected condition. In medieval times and for three centuries afterwards, it had been a valued asset on which the townspeople had freely grazed their animals, but in the eighteenth century it had become an anachronism. The Town Fields and the Town Moor had been designed for very different social conditions from those which now prevailed. People were no longer content to live off the land, growing their own food and making their own clothes; in a more commercial age, most workers had become wage-earners in various jobs, especially in urban-based industries, and were accustomed to thinking in terms of money rather than manorial privileges. Moreover, a greatly increased population required a more scientific approach to agriculture so that more food could be grown than was possible under the old system of open grazing and strip cultivation in open fields.

The solution to the problem was to abandon the open system of farming and divide the Town Fields and Town Moor into separate smaller fields, each enclosed with its own fences, walls, or hedges. In a piecemeal way, in different parts of the country, this had been happening in past centuries, as the peasant-farmer who had worked on manorial fields was 'bought out' by his feudal lord or by rich burgesses; a new class of farmers known as yeomen had long been farming enclosed fields, and country squires had not only farmed their own fields in this way but also rented some of their fields to tenant farmers. In the eighteenth century the enclosure system became a matter of national policy, and large areas of common lands belonging to townships and manors were turned into numerous smaller fields by a succession of Enclosure Acts.

Meanwhile Barnard Castle's own Town Moor had fallen into neglect through being under-used. By 1784 it was said that not one poor man kept a cow on the Town

Moor. It was still used for sheep, however, and also for some strings of Scotch Galloways (a strong and hardy breed of horses) from which half-a-dozen men gained a livelihood. A few people each grazed a horse on it and used the animal for hauling coal from Copley, six miles (9.5km) away. From time to time a few short-horned cattle were put on it without much benefit to themselves or the owner.

The Moor was in a poor condition. The soil was undernourished, there were many acres that were stony and, where drainage was poor, there were large areas where only rushes grew. Other parts were covered in furze, which could only be destroyed by burning and then spreading lime over the scorched earth. As early as 1754, consideration was given to 'enclosing' the Town Moor, and a survey of great care and thoughtfulness was conducted by Thomas Colpitts, a surveyor, who concluded that the whole exercise of enclosing such unsuitable land would not be worth the expenditure involved.

The Town Fields and the Town Pasture presented less of a problem for enclosure, and they and a few other parcels of land were divided into enclosed fields in 1783. The task of enclosing the Town Moor was begun in 1795, despite the advice which Mr Colpitts had given forty years earlier. Eventually, about 4,000 acres (1,600ha) of the Town Moor were divided into fields, following surveyor's plans which had been drawn up by George Dixon, brother of the distinguished Jeremiah Dixon who was one of the two surveyors who created the Mason-Dixon line in America. (The Dixon family lived in the village of Cockfield, eight miles (13km) from Barnard Castle.) The Little Moor, which lay to the east of the town, was enclosed in 1799, completing the enclosure of Barnard Castle's 'open' fields.

Enclosed fields to the east of the town: the land in the foreground was once part of the Little Moor, and the fields sloping towards it cover parts of the former New Field and Town Pasture.

The entrance to the first farm built on the old Town Pasture. The farm's white walls
indicate that it is part of the Raby estate.

After the Enclosure Acts the town's surroundings acquired the appearance which
they have today, with fields neatly divided by hawthorn hedges or, where stone was
readily available, by drystone walls. Farmhouses began to appear where several fields
were owned or rented by one man; those that belonged to the Raby estate were whitewashed and the others were left in their natural colour. Most of the many roads which
now cross the countryside were newly created or at least greatly improved to give access
to fields and farms situated in areas that had once been reached simply by going at
random across common land. The first new farmhouse was built on the old Town
Pasture and was called Town Pasture Farm — a name which had to be changed to East
Town Pasture when another farm was built nearby and named West Town Pasture; they
both stood near a new road, Town Pasture Lane, which links the Bishop Auckland and
Darlington roads. So the name of the old system was preserved in the new.

Enclosure had a mixed effect on Barnard Castle. In some ways it became a more
flourishing town, partly because the new roads encouraged people to travel into their
market centre and partly because the rural population living in outlying farmhouses
had grown. A surprisingly large number of the new fields became arable, even on the
higher and more wind-swept countryside that had been the Town Moor. In 1840
almost half of all fields below 900 feet (275m) above sea level were ploughed, and the
whole of Barnard Castle's enclosed area was at less than that height. Very many of the
fields that are pasture in the twentieth century were once arable, which greatly
enhanced Barnard Castle's importance as a corn market town. On the other hand,
enclosure was one of the factors that led to the end of the town's annual fairs. The
common lands (referred to sometimes as 'waste lands') had supplied free pasturage
for the cattle, sheep and horses which were brought for sale at the fairs. Without this

facility the fairs dwindled and did not last long into the nineteenth century, though they were later temporarily revived.

The effect of enclosure on the people themselves was also mixed. The lifestyle of many countrymen changed for the worse. From farming small areas of land under their own initiative, they found themselves working for richer men who farmed the newly-created fields; some were kept busy at first by erecting walls or planting hedges, but such work was only temporary, for the same walls lasted with minor repairs for 200 years. These men lost their sense of independence; hirings days became more significant as the workers looked for new farming jobs; some who failed to find agricultural work drifted into larger towns to seek work in industry; others stayed in their home town and became a burden on the Poor Law system. The number of paupers in Barnard Castle's poor house trebled between 1762, when there were 20 inmates, and 1834 when there were 65.

Enclosure had, however, increased the amount of money that was available for helping the poor. Some of the income for charitable purposes had previously been raised by renting out pieces of land which had been bequeathed for the purpose. When these pieces were sold to be enclosed, the small annual income was replaced by a capital sum which proved useful in, for example, discharging the mortgage on the poor house. Interest on the remaining capital was used to provide 'outside relief' to people living outside the poor house.

St John's Hospital in Newgate did not benefit from the enclosure system; the hospital's right to use parts of the Town Fields had been complicated and when the Enclosure Act was applied, the hospital was given some plots of land in lieu of its ancient rights of mowing and grazing. Unfortunately the master of the hospital (who was also the curate-in-charge of St Mary's) did not ensure that the plots were properly fenced, which later led to administrative difficulties. Moreover, the master had some years earlier rented out the hospital's lands and privileges on long-term leases; this may have made administration easier for him, but it was not profitable. Three people took out leases for their own lifetimes, and as their ages were 29, 22 and 18 the leases ran for a very long time, during which the value of the land increased while the hospital gained no additional benefits. The youngest lessee died at the age of eight-five, by which time the hospital had lost many hundreds of pounds. By 1815 there were only two bedeswomen, the thatch on the building had turned brown with age, and one townsman said that the hospital looked like a humble shed. In 1863, when the last lessee died, there was only one bedeswoman and part of the roof had fallen in.

The master of the hospital was responsible for paying allowances to the bedeswomen and paying for the maintenance of the building; after that, the rest of the hospital's income was his own, as his payment for administering the charity. The deterioration of the standards of administration of ancient charities was by no means unique to Barnard Castle. Anthony Trollope's novel *The Warden*, published in 1855, has as its main theme the improper administration of a similar charity, and the author comments, 'such matters have begun to be talked of in various parts of England ... men are beginning to say that these things must be looked into'.

The people of Barnard Castle were no exception; they wanted an examination of the affairs of St John's Hospital. In 1829 the national commissioners who enquired into the state of charities published a report which echoed the townspeople's concern. They forbade the issue of further leases when the current ones expired. This first took effect in 1837. On the expiry of the last lease, in 1863, the townspeople (with the consent of the master) obtained a ruling from the Court of Chancery that, on the

In a collection of unpublished papers this building is described as the 'old Poor House', but it may possibly depict St John's Hospital. Both buildings were in a very unsound condition.

death or resignation of the present master, the affairs of the hospital were to be conducted by twelve trustees who were to restore the number of bedeswomen to three, to rebuild the hospital, and to divert other funds to an entirely new project — namely, the creation of a grammar school in the town.

The master of the hospital died in 1865, and the trustees began their task under the chairmanship of the new vicar. (In that year Barnard Castle had become a parish, instead of being a part of the parish of Gainford.) The trustees identified all hospital lands and fenced and drained them, but did not manage to rebuild the hospital or make any progress towards establishing a grammar school.

The town's official poor house was in much the same state of disrepair as St John's Hospital. Children, as well as adults, lived in the dilapidated building; the children attended the National school in the town until they were eight years old, and able-bodied adult paupers were expected to work for the township on the roads or in the town quarry, or to do other manual work such as cleaning the streets, before returning to the poor house at night. Other inmates worked at the three weaving looms and a warping mill in the building, or worked in the adjacent kitchen garden.

The Poor Law Amendment Act of 1834 severely lessened the amount of 'outdoor relief' given to the poor, and made new workhouses a central feature of its administration. Conditions in the workhouses were intentionally made unpleasant to discourage poor people from entering the building unless they were desperate. Since, however, there was less outdoor relief, many more paupers did move into the dreaded workhouses. This called for bigger buildings, so to spread the cost more evenly among those paying the poor rate, neighbouring parishes were combined to form unions. The scheme disregarded county boundaries, and the Teesdale Union consisted of

An eighteenth century engraving indicating that the Tees was navigable by small boats.

The 'Hermit of Barnard Castle' strolls in his garden within the castle walls. From an etching published in 1845. *(See page 65.)*

nearly 175,000 acres (71,000ha), of which about 96,000 (39,000ha) were in Yorkshire. It was divided into sub-districts, of which Barnard Castle was one.

Long before the whole scheme was completed, a large workhouse was built at the top of Galgate, opposite the two thatched cottages that had been built in the eighteenth century, but otherwise in the open countryside. Erected in 1838, it was a long stone building separated from the road by lawns and trees. It was unpretentious and even quietly dignified, unlike some of the ornate and imposing workhouses later built in other towns. A series of rooms, based on a plan of four quadrangles, included a room for 'old men', another for 'boys' and two sitting-rooms for 'able men'. On the opposite wing, in a different quadrangle, were equivalent rooms for women. Even husbands and wives were segregated from each other. In the remote corners of the two larger quadrangles were rooms known as the men's and women's 'refractory rooms' where inmates were imprisoned for breaches of discipline. Another room, situated against the outer wall of the buildings, was the mortuary or 'dead room', and there were also two rooms for, respectively, female and male vagrants. These were people who 'tramped' on a more or less predetermined circuit through the northern countryside and either slept rough or took refuge overnight in workhouses. In the very centre of the complex was the master's residence (his wife was usually the matron), and at the front of the building was the board room in which a large committee known as the Board of Guardians periodically met and made decisions about policy and practical issues at a local level. The workhouse system for the whole country was controlled by a team of commissioners and regional officers.

The establishment lived up to its full title of the Teesdale Union Workhouse, for the 'able' inmates worked in and about the building: the women performed kitchen and laundry duties, and scrubbed the long stone-flagged corridors; and the men worked in the large kitchen gardens, chopped wood, carried coals, cleaned outside windows and presumably emptied the twenty earth closets and attended to the pigs which were kept near the kitchen gardens and whose effluent ran into the drain known as Bartholomews Dyke, which flowed down beside the Back Lane. Children who had attended the National school could be apprenticed for seven years to learn a trade, and some children worked in the textile mills in Bridgegate. The children were not necessarily related to the inmates of the workhouse, for part of the duties of the overseers of the poor was the care of illegitimate children if they were not otherwise adequately cared for. The reduced amount of outdoor relief and the frugal lifestyle within the workhouse helped to satisfy contributors to the poor rate, whatever it did to the needy.

Fortunately, various voluntary organisations began to make provision for the spiritual, mental and physical care of Barnard Castle, including its poor. This new wave of care for the inhabitants was very timely because the growth of the densely-populated industrial area in the lower part of the town had created a social problem. In addition to the flax mill downstream from the town and Ullathornes Mill upstream on the opposite bank, carpet and woollen mills now lined the whole riverside from Thorngate to the County Bridge, and the workers' housing conditions were cramped, airless and insanitary. As well as the mills themselves, the area contained buildings which were used by related industries such as dyeing, while in forges and carpenters' shops men worked at making and mending parts of the machinery used in the mills.

The manufacture of carpets had been started in Barnard Castle by Thomas Crampton who, despite his commercial initiative, ended his days in the workhouse. In the time of his prosperity, however, other mill-owners had followed his lead and

Some of the factories which lined the riverside of Bridgegate.

produced carpets in the style of Kidderminster and, to some extent, Brussels (with a looped pile), and Venetian carpet which was used on flights of stairs. The typical Barnard Castle carpet was created in strips which were sewn together to the size and shape required. They had no pile and were reversible, with the same pattern on each side, though the colours on one side were the reverse of the other. The pattern was geometric in style, sometimes with formalised flowers in quite bright colours. It was the kind of product that is now generally called Welsh tapestry.

By 1827 there were five or six carpet factories, and in 1851 some carpets from Barnard Castle were exhibited in the Great Exhibition in the Crystal Palace in London. The factories employed several hundred people, some of them on intermittent spells of labour. Most of the local manufacturers did not spin their own materials but imported them from Yorkshire mills. However, the firm of Monkhouse and Whitfield did its own spinning as well as weaving, and employed over 200 people. Some weavers dyed their wool themselves, while others used dye-vats that were located on the riverbank beside Richard Dunn's carpet factory. Materials for dyeing were taken in and out of doorways that faced onto the river and were then conveyed in rowing boats up and down the stretch of river that was lined with factories; sometimes sails may have been used if the wind was favourable. This procedure was easier and quicker than loading and unloading carts to be pulled by horses through the narrow street of Bridgegate.

The 'yards' that ran at right-angles to the street were in some cases little more than alleyways between tall factory buildings; on both sides of the street the large eighteenth century houses, as well as some smaller dwellings, had become tenements. Sometimes four or even five families shared one big room subdivided only by curtains, affording

53

a meagre degree of privacy but doing nothing to combat the stale, unhealthy air. In Thorngate itself, very little air blew off the river, partly because the prevailing winds were easterly or westerly, but chiefly because there was only a narrow riverside gap between two big factories. In 1846 J Monkhouse and Sons built a long three-storey mill on the east of Thorngate, replacing houses and gardens, and further reducing the fresh air and sunshine that entered the street. Several even more airless yards ran off the sides of Thorngate leading to dwellings behind the large houses.

The situation was worsened by the appalling lack of adequate sanitary arrangements for a rapidly increasing population. Little extra provision had been made when wealthy families and their servants moved out of the big houses to be replaced by industrial workers in much greater numbers. The number of earth closets hardly increased and there were open cesspits in the centre of the widest parts of the enclosed yards, in close proximity to the workers' cottages that were reached through the narrow alleyways.

The Kings Head, where Charles Dickens stayed and recommended the ale. The premises were recently renamed after the author. *(See page 62.)*

The carpet factory which was built onto this eighteenth century house extended to the river.

A view from the opposite riverbank, showing the loading door facing onto the river.

Some level of industrial work had always been a feature of Barnard Castle, but the scale on which it had now developed was alien to the traditional nature of the town. In fact industry had almost created another and different town, adjacent to the old one: the market town existed above the Market Cross, but a new industrial town had sprung up beside the river. More and more workers and their families came to the factories, not only from the neighbourhood, but from quite distant towns such as Kidderminster where the carpet trade had given workers experience which they hoped would be advantageous to them in the new factories in Barnard Castle. The population increased so quickly and in such an unsuitable area that the town authorities, with their limited powers, were quite unable to cope with the complex situation.

In 1801 there had been 2,966 people living in Barnard Castle, and ten years later there were only 20 more, but in the next twenty years the population rose from 2,986 to 3,581 in 1821, and to 4,430 in 1831. In 1821, there were 626 families whose main income came from working in the factories, while only 94 families were mainly dependent on agriculture. One in four of the carpet-weavers occupied, with their families, single-room tenements. Except for a few who lived in yards off the Horse Market and the Market Place, all the workers and their families lived below the Market Cross.

The lower end of the town was quite notorious for its low level of existence, not only from the point of view of physical well-being but also for its moral laxity and criminal tendencies. In a poem entitled *Castle - Barnard*, published in 1823, its author G Layton conducts the reader on an imaginary tour of the town. Here are two stanzas on Bridgegate:

Next Bridgegate comes, all Barnard's muddy sink
Where reigns, supremely great, the god of s..nk:
Thy crimes unseemly would disgrace my lay,
So let them sleep nor see the light of day.

With hasty steps, I skim the pest-rife street,
Anxious to 'scape the noxious gales I meet
From tan-pits, puddles, filthy refuse, worse —
The whole might rival ancient Egypt's curse.

Mr Layton was anxious to turn away from the troubles of the area, but there were other people who took a more helpful view of the town's social problems. First, they approached the situation from a religious and educational viewpoint. In 1821 hundreds of people gathered to listen to a speaker on Primitive Methodism, and a group of nine local supporters began to form a church in Barnard Castle; within six months they had 120 members. Their first place of worship was a former weavers' shop off Gray Lane; it was a two-storey building and the 'Primitives' cut a large hole in the ceiling of the ground floor so that the upper storey became a sort of gallery, with the preacher standing below in a pulpit which, much later, was jocularly said to have looked like a large beer barrel. So successful was the movement that in 1828 the members began to erect a purpose-built chapel in one of the yards which ran from the Bank to the Demesnes; the yard became known as Ranters Yard from the enthusiastic style in which the services were conducted. The new chapel seated 500 people and the Sunday school had 150 pupils.

The Wesleyans had also expanded, and in 1823 left their Broadgates chapel in favour of a new one in a spacious yard off the Bank. It included a tiered gallery supported by iron pillars and had a total capacity for 1,000 people.

The industrial area almost formed another town.

Sunday schools and day schools accompanied these developments. The pioneering movement was the 'Independent Congregation of Protestant Dissenters' (later known as the Congregational Church), who began a Sunday school in Newgate in 1803 and moved to larger premises in the Market Place in 1811, before using a room in the Wesleyan chapel in Broadgates. A few years later the Congregationalists had a church in Newgate, and thrived so well that by 1836 they had built a new church seating 400 people and having an adjoining schoolroom. This time, they chose the old Back Lane as a site, there being little land available in the more populated area of the town. In this case industry followed the school, for the Back Lane was soon to

Inside the entrance to Ranters Yard, facing towards the Bank.

Barnard Castle's first National school.

become Barnard Castle's second industrial area. In 1839 the Wesleyans created a day school for boys and girls at the lower end of the Demesnes, which usefully augmented an infants school that had been erected at the top of the slope by the British and Foreign School Society, a Nonconformist organisation similar to the National Society which built schools to foster education on Anglican principles. The latter society had built a National school in Barnard Castle in 1814 at the south-east corner of the churchyard. It was not an impressive building, but it did accommodate 150 pupils and was the first purpose-built school in the town.

In the midst of all this progress, St Mary's Church itself was in a very poor condition. No work seemed to have been done to the fabric for many years. In Hutchinson's *History* the author does not mince his words: 'The inside', he writes, 'is wretchedly stalled, the pavement broken and uneven, and the whole appearance slovenly and offensive.' The source of much of this situation was that burials were still being conducted inside the church. The 'stalls' (or pews) were movable and temporarily cleared from the area where a new grave was to be dug; the disturbed soil containing the remains of previous burials caused an unwholesome smell to hang in the air. Some renovation was carried out in 1814, and the south wall of the chancel was rebuilt with one large window instead of four small ones. The interior was whitewashed to lighten the building, but the ceiling was of dark oak, and two large galleries, one of which overhung forty-one feet (12.5m) of the nave, cast shadows and obscured a view of the service from some parts of the church, while also worsening the acoustics. In 1823 a barrel organ was installed and six bells were hung in the tower, but the church was in need of much more stringent renovation.

Apart from schools and chapels, other organisations were established in this period, all aiming to improve some aspect of local life. Barnard Castle was one of the first towns in England to have an agricultural society, and annual shows were held in the field behind the Kings Head. With a more general purpose, a subscription library was opened in 1824 with over 100 subscribing members, but it did not last long and was superseded by a mechanics institute which aimed to provide education for adult workers so that they might, perhaps, better their prospects at work and, in any case, lead fuller lives. By 1839 it owned 450 books, as well as mineral specimens and ten working models of industrial mechanical processes; there were also models to show the solar system, and various other pieces of scientific equipment. The mechanics institute at Barnard Castle was founded by H T M Witham Esq, a philanthropist who lived at Lartington Hall about two miles (3km) away. In his lifetime the institute had only rented accommodation, but after he died a Witham Testimonial building was erected in his memory by public donations and became the permanent centre of the mechanics institute.

The building also included the headquarters of the Barnard Castle Dispensary for the Relief of the Sick Poor; its scheme was to offer advice and medicine to the poor, free of charge. Its president was the duke of Cleveland, a title acquired by the third earl of Darlington in 1833. The 'Dispensary', as it was generally called, was a very important element in the town's life. In its first year when it (like the 'Mechanics') was in temporary accommodation it helped 175 patients, and it increased its activities until, towards the end of the century, it helped up to 300 patients a year. It did particularly valuable work during periods of industrial and trade depression in the town, as in 1841 when the poorest classes were in 'want of proper food and clothing'; in that year the annual report of the society revealed that 176 patients had been cured, 15 had died, and 26 were 'still on the books'. The society also had a room in the Witham Testimonial for any patient who lived outside the town but who had undergone surgery and was not yet fit to go home.

The dignified classical frontage of the Witham Testimonial lent a new air of distinction to the curve of the Horse Market and the Market Place, which had already been improved by the demolition of the old tollbooth in 1808. It had become increasingly unattractive, being spattered with mud and other stains, and surrounded by rubbish and broken butchers' stalls, and people were beginning to feel that the Market Place was unhealthy; they thought that both the Butter Market and the tollbooth hindered a free flow of air through the street, and the shambles (which were part of the tollbooth building) added to the unpleasant smell that characterised the area. After the tollbooth and shambles were demolished, an immediate improvement was noticed in this respect.

Some of the functions of the old tollbooth were taken over by the Butter Market, which is referred to in the Vestry minutes as the Town Hall. A courtroom was built within its upper storey in 1814, and the court of petty sessions was held there. In 1826 a small gallery was added for the jury, reached by a short staircase with a little door at which the constable stood on guard, and the whole room was given more dignity by a large stone carving, let into the wall, of the arms of the Vane family, the lords of the manor. The Butter Market had entered a new lease of life, and the stone tablet on the outside recording Thomas Breaks' gift to the town was repainted through the individual

The Butter Market still stands in a dominant position in the town centre.

efforts of a local 'character' called Bobby Dalkin. As the functions of the Butter Market increased, the building was more commonly referred to as the Market Cross.

It was all very different from some people's attitude to the Butter Market a few years earlier. The building had been referred to as 'Breaks' Folly' and regarded as an obstruction to the free flow of both air and traffic, and as a visual obstruction to the pleasing curve of the market streets and the Bank. In 1804 two marksmen had even used its weather vane as a target to prove who was the better shot. From outside the Turks Head, the first shot hit the vane and swung it round, and the second hit it and swung it back to its original position. Had this escapade taken place half a dozen years later the men might have been incarcerated in the Market Cross, for the central part of the ground floor was walled up to create a cell for prisoners awaiting trial in the courtroom above.

The annual fairs, though soon to disappear, were still being proclaimed with ancient ceremony. A procession of the town's officials started at the Market Cross and then perambulated the boundaries of the fair. First came the bailiff, carrying a white wand, followed by the town constables, carrying equipment from the town armoury, including halberds and batons. (No-one else was allowed to carry weapons on fair days.) They were followed by market and fair officials, and they all marched from the Market Cross into Galgate, to Cripple Hill (the slope at the top of which Marshall Street now stands), and returned and walked down into Thorngate. At each of these three points they proclaimed the rules of the fair: no cattle or goods could be sold outside the route which they had followed. Some form of music accompanied the officials, and from all over Teesdale people arrived in their best clothes to enjoy the festive atmosphere as well as to inspect the stalls, peddlers' wares and the livestock.

From such an auspicious start, the day often deteriorated into misbehaviour involving fights between the townsmen and visiting men from upper Teesdale. There was an ancient feud between the two groups. The upper dalesmen were quarrymen, leadminers and farmers, and they spoke derisively of 'the poor silly weavers o' Barney Castle'. The latter referred to the dalesmen as 'Heelanders', suggesting they were like the rough Border raiders of old. In fact, the dalesmen did come in gangs down the valley, and in the fights that ensued they usually came off best. An eyewitness commented:

> The Barnard Castle weavers were no match for the stout, healthy, brawny lads of Mickleton, Middleton, Forest and Frith; ... it was no uncommon occurrence to see at least three, to as many as six weavers, all set, like as many butchers' dogs, upon one Heelander, who often proved the conqueror.

Sometimes the weavers felt that they had a strong enough army to go up the valley on Middleton Fair Day and carry the fight onto their adversaries' home ground, but they were invariably defeated and came back wounded and bloody, sometimes with broken bones.

On Whit Wednesday 1816 there was a tremendous fight in the Market Place at Barnard Castle. Heavy bludgeons were used, stalls were smashed and overthrown, and broadcloth, cheeses, gingerbread, hats, hardware, fruit and various other articles offered for sale were scattered about and trampled underfoot. Shopkeepers closed their premises, and visiting showmen packed up their exhibits and began to move their caravans out of the way as speedily as possible. Cattle and sheep, freed from their pens, ran wildly about the town. Two of the 'Heelanders' were arrested and locked in the 'Black Hole', the name given to the cell in the ground floor of the Market Cross. On the following day the miners from upper Teesdale assembled in great force and began to march down to Barnard Castle to free the prisoners. The militia was called out to restore order, and the magistrates, as an additional safeguard against further trouble, ordered the release of the two men, and the disturbance ended.

Those who enjoyed fighting against rival factions were given new opportunities when, following the 1832 Reform Act, Barnard Castle became a polling station for South West Durham during Parliamentary elections. There are strong indications that mobs were paid by candidates either for their support or for opposing the candidate's political rivals. A Yorkshireman who was a Conservative candidate in Barnard Castle in 1841 was conveyed enthusiastically through the streets by men who went between the shafts of his carriage while others cheered them on, but a newspaper report claimed that if the men had been paid a shilling more by the other side, they would have tipped the candidate into the Tees. Rival mobs howled down various candidates who were making speeches and when, six years later, the man who had been triumphantly paraded through the streets returned to Barnard Castle he was pelted with bread and herrings. When he retreated, the mob cheered for Mr John Bowes of Streatlam Castle, who had been successful at an earlier election but was not even a candidate on the present occasion and was, in fact, on holiday in Paris. The disorderly mob having, for the moment, no other activity in mind then threw mud and stones at a local doctor who happened to be walking up the street, until he took refuge in a nearby house.

Apart from fairs and elections, other special occasions gave a more acceptable outlet for displays of public feeling. A whole ox was publicly roasted in Barnard Castle in 1809 on the twenty-first birthday of Lord Barnard, eldest son of the earl of Darlington; and in 1831 the coronation of William IV and Queen Adelaide was celebrated in the town by a magnificent display of Chinese fireworks with festivities lasting from eight o'clock in the evening until half past eleven. Six years later the coronation of Queen Victoria was formally proclaimed at 'the usual places' in the town (probably the same points at which fairs were proclaimed), flags were flown and the church bells rang.

Other talking points during this period included the visits of leading literary and artistic figures. In 1809 Sir Walter Scott paid the first of his visits to Rokeby (three miles/5km away) which became the title of a long poem published in 1813, extolling the beauties of Teesdale and telling a story which begins with a guard pacing the top of the round tower of Barnard Castle. The poem had an immense impact on Teesdale and Barnard Castle, for it made the area so famous that, almost single-handed, Scott founded the local tourist industry. When the railway came much later in the century, it brought great numbers of travellers who still wanted to follow in Scott's footsteps. In 1816 and 1818 the great artist J M W Turner visited Barnard Castle and rode through Teesdale. His paintings increased the fame of the area, especially when engravings from his works were used as illustrations in later editions of Scott's poetry.

Sir Walter Scott is said to have composed part of his poem *Rokeby* in this grotto, in private grounds overlooking the River Greta.

Another literary figure whose visit created much interest was Charles Dickens, who stayed for two nights at the Kings Head Hotel in 1838. He was already a well-known novelist, having written *The Pickwick Papers* and most of *Oliver Twist* in serial instalments. He was in Barnard Castle to research for *Nicholas Nickleby*, in which he was to satirise Yorkshire boarding schools under the fictitious name of 'Dotheboys Hall'. The school of William Shaw at Bowes, four miles (6.5km) from Barnard Castle,

This building at Bowes, formerly William Shaw's Academy, is generally believed to be the original of 'Dotheboys Hall'.

has generally been accepted as the prototype for Dickens' satire, and he interviewed people at Bowes and at Barnard Castle in order to gain an impression of how the pupils lived in such establishments.

The town also gave him the title for *Master Humphrey's Clock*, named after the shop of Thomas Humphreys, a clock-maker who was a native of Barnard Castle and who had premises at the corner of Newgate and the Bank. Among various local references in Dickens' works there is a gratuitous advertisement for the Kings Head in a letter from Newman Noggs, a character in *Nicholas Nickleby*, which ends 'p.s. — If you should go near Barnard Castle, there is good ale at the King's Head'.

Barnard Castle was well supplied with inns and public houses; in the first half of the nineteenth century there were between 25 and 30, spread throughout the streets, though mainly concentrated on the Market Place. Many of these establishments provided entertainments for visitors and residents alike. The Queens Head continued to flourish and had a very large room called Prickett's Long Room, after the name of the proprietor. It was used as a theatre and in 1806 Edmund Kean, destined to become one of England's greatest actors, put on a one-man show there, including excerpts from *Richard III*, a role in which he later became famous on the London stage. Sometimes local amateurs who fancied acting with professional touring companies were given small parts in productions at the Queens Head. A touring conjuror was another attraction. Balls, wedding receptions and other public occasions took place at the same inn, with visitors alighting from their carriages in the inn yard, which was reached from Newgate though the inn faced onto the Market Place.

Theatrical companies sometimes performed in other public houses, even using premises that had earlier been cockpits, behind the Red Lion and the Raby Hotel on opposite sides of the Market Place. There was only one purpose-built theatre, which opened in 1832 with a performance presented by the Richmond Theatre Company.

Women fishing in the Tees.

The venture did not last long, and in 1840 the building, on the south side of the churchyard was bought by the managers of the National school for the girls' department.

This was a period when organised country pursuits were being established. In 1832 Barnard Castle Cricket Club was founded, playing its matches at Woolhouse Farm, outside the town. Fox-hunting was popular for those who could afford it and for others who enjoyed the spectacle; the then earl of Darlington had founded a pack of hounds at Raby in 1787 for his enthusiastic son who, when he succeeded the earl, developed it into a first-class hunt which he maintained for over fifty years. Frequent meets were held near Barnard Castle. Fishing was well established as a local sport, and several pictures of the period show both men and women angling in the Tees, as well as men fishing from boats for salmon. These men must sometimes have been disappointed for, in 1820, Robert Surtees, the historian, complained that there were fewer salmon in the Tees, because of 'the pernicious effects of the lead mines on the higher streams'.

In all kinds of ways the town had become a lively and prosperous place, not just as a market town but as a trading centre for manufacturers of a wide variety of goods. There were clock-makers, numerous shoe-makers, craftsmen in brass and iron, furniture makers, confectioners and bakers (some specialising in gingerbread), and, listed in a directory of 1827, over a dozen proprietors of private schools, for which no formal qualifications were needed.

It was the age of the entrepreneur, when men or women who had failed at one trade or profession were willing to try another and who seized on any available premises in which to conduct it. In 1822 a sawmill was established on the north bank of the Tees; its partners had previously been a plumber, a hosier, and a baker, but their work-force seemed to turn out quite sophisticated articles. At about the same time the castle was used as a factory for producing lead shot. The round tower was used for casting round shot by the method of dropping molten lead from the top into a bath of water below. Some people objected to a small superstructure that was built on top of the tower, but others felt that the use of the castle as a factory helped to keep it in good condition, as the proprietor had repaired part of the walls for his purpose.

About twenty years later the castle was again inhabited but by only one man, known as the Hermit of Barnard Castle. He was Francis (Frank) Shields, and he used the round tower and an adjacent room as a house, and cultivated the area at the base of the Great Hall as a neat vegetable garden (see page 51). He lived there for twenty years, was described as 'castle-keeper' in a directory of 1851, and acted as a guide to the castle. One of his visitors was Charles Dodgson, later to become famous as Lewis Carroll, the author of *Alice in Wonderland*.

Frank Shields, castle-keeper, poses for a portrait by a local photographer.

Parts of the outer walls of the castle were in poor condition. In 1818 a section of the wall on the Bridgegate side fell; it broke down the roof of a house, and a man working in a saw-pit owed his life to a tree trunk lying above him which sheltered him from the falling stones. Another lucky escape occurred in 1827 when, in the early hours of the morning, a huge rock fell from the castle cliff and struck another house in Bridgegate, wrecking a bedroom in which two men were sleeping and burying two children in the room below under the debris. All escaped alive.

It is difficult to avoid the thought that the situation might have been remedied if it had threatened any other street. Bridgegate remained neglected while efforts were being made to improve the rest of the town.

A subscription list was opened for improvement schemes, and the Market Place was cleaned and paving stones were laid on each side. In 1823 G Layton wrote: 'Great improvements have taken place. A new street, called King Street is now building. The other streets have undergone

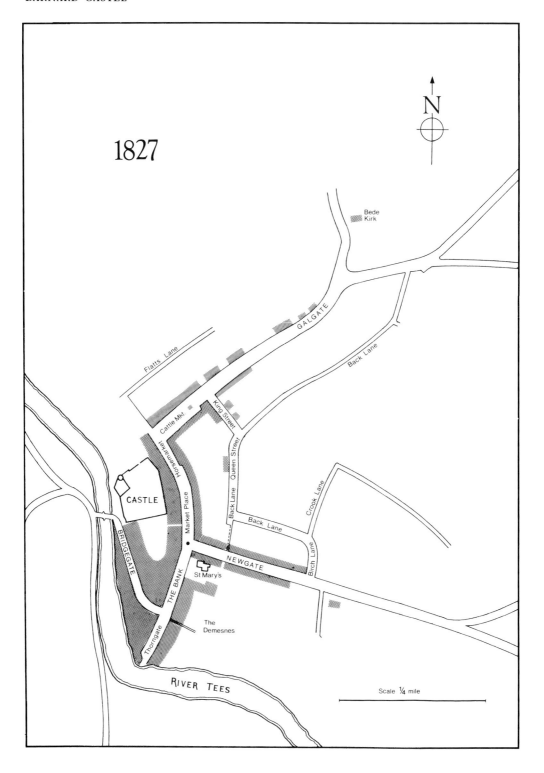

1827

N

Bede Kirk

GALGATE

Flatts Lane

Back Lane

Cattle Mkt.

King Street

Horsemarket

Queen Street

Back Lane

Crook Lane

CASTLE

Market Place

Back Lane

NEWGATE

Birch Lane

BRIDGEGATE

THE BANK

St Mary's

Thorngate

The Demesnes

RIVER TEES

Scale ¼ mile

The heckling shops in Queen Street were still in industrial use in 1997.

considerable repairs.' A town map of 1827 shows thirteen houses in King Street; the side which joined upper Galgate had dignified houses with gardens behind and between them, and there were smaller houses opposite. The street linked Galgate with the old Back Lane, where a row of small houses was built. The two streets were named King Street and Queen Street, after George IV and Queen Caroline.

At this time industrial development began to appear around Queen Street. The riverside was already over-built and the Back Lane gave ready-made access to new sites for industries that had no need for water power. A foundry was built behind the row of houses in Queen Street, and the firm of Ullathorne, who owned the flax mill at Bridge End, built a new workshop in which to comb out the strands of the flax, a process known as 'hackling' or 'heckling'. The new building was called the Heckling Shop and was built at the lower end of the Back Lane at the junction of what are now Birch Road and Queen Street. The workers were housed in Hecklers Row which was situated on the less prosperous side of King Street. The backs of these houses formed one side of Portland Square — which sounds rather grand but was so named because the owner of the property was an agent for Portland Cement.

Before the middle of the nineteenth century short streets, such as George Street, Ware Street and Hall Street, began to fill in the space between the Back Lane and the Horse Market. The houses were purpose-built for the workers in the succession of industries which sprang up nearby. These included another foundry, three smithies, a rope works, a saw-pit, a bakery, a malt house and a guano warehouse; quite a large space was left vacant round this particular building, probably because of the foul smell of the guano, a fertiliser made from fish and the excrement of sea birds.

All these little streets were an immense improvement on Bridgegate, because they were provided with adequate sanitation, and fitted the purpose for which they had been built. The Congregational church had already been built in this area, in 1836, and by 1848 the Roman Catholics had their first church in Barnard Castle in Ware Street, which ran parallel to Hall Street where the Congregationalists met. Each church had a schoolroom and the Roman Catholics built a presbytery which opened onto Queen Street. Hitherto their nearest priests and churches had been at Lartington, two miles (3km) away, and at Hutton Magna, six miles (9.5km) away.

Of the other streets in the town, today's Birch Road was a country lane containing one short row of houses, but Newgate had houses on both sides, the more wealthy and dignified examples being at the end farthest from the town. At the narrow entry

near the Market Cross, the houses were in as bad a condition as St John's Hospital and were described as 'ruinous', but at the wider part of the street new houses were built in 1826 in a quietly dignified style, and at the eastern entry to the street Mr William Watson built Spring Lodge in 1825. It stood in large grounds laid out as garden and parkland, and within two years it was guaranteed further seclusion by trees which were planted along its Newgate frontage and down Demesnes Lane. The town's most affluent property owners had houses in Thorngate, Newgate and Galgate, though some of their near neighbours were not at all wealthy. The most noticeable of these houses, because it stood actually in the middle of the road, was one belonging to Sir Clifford Constable at the entry to the cattle market in Galgate.

Houses built in 1826 added quiet dignity to the street of Newgate.

The site chosen for one of the town's biggest industrial buildings was equally surprising, for the gas works were built among the trees on the wooded banks of the Tees just upstream of the castle, and while the foundations were being extended, the remains of a Roman road were discovered beside the site of the early river-crossing. The gas works buildings were 160 yards (145m) long and included two iron gas holders. Work on their construction started in 1835 and soon influenced the town. St Mary's Church was lit by gas by 1839 and in the 1840s the town had eighty-two gas lamps in its streets. This beneficial industry was conducted

The archways on the left of this photograph of western Bridgegate led to enclosed yards which extended right up to the castle cliff. All the houses on that side of the street have since been demolished.

out of sight of the town, without any harmful effect on the health of the people, and without any adverse impact on the housing situation.

In these respects it was quite unlike the industrial riverside development downstream of the castle. Bridgegate, Thorngate and the Bank were on the brink of tragedy: they were about to be engulfed in the darkest period in the history of Barnard Castle.

The dreadful illness known as Asiatic cholera struck Barnard Castle in 1847 and 1849. The reason for the spread and the recurrence of the disease was unhealthy living conditions, a polluted water supply and the absence of any national legislation for improving the situation. Apart from overcrowding and grossly inadequate sanitary conditions, Barnard Castle's troubles were increased by the tanning industry which used human urine in part of its process, and sometimes abandoned its unwanted tan-pits to be used as unofficial receptacles for rubbish of all kinds. Slaughter houses were uncontrolled until 1851, and the disposal of unwanted parts of the carcasses was carried out in a random way. In many of the enclosed yards of the town, pigs, cows and hens were kept among the tenements inhabited by human beings, and the dung heaps contained both human and animal excrement, and parts of slaughtered animals.

During and after the 1847 outbreak of cholera, it was left to the guardians of the Teesdale Union to attempt to improve some of the most unhealthy conditions, but they had no real power to make their efforts effective, and when in 1849 a much worse outbreak occurred they could only light bonfires in the streets to fumigate the area and diminish the smell which hung in the air. Doctors did what they could for the sick, often breaking window panes with towels wrapped round their fists to ventilate rooms where people lay ill or dying, and the curate-in-charge of St Mary's Church, the Reverend George Dugard, was brave and industrious in visiting the stricken houses to minister to the sick and dying and to comfort the bereaved.

During the 1849 epidemic, 369 people caught cholera, and there were 1,297 cases of premonitory diarrhoea which did not fully develop into cholera. Within one period of eight weeks, 145 of the victims died. The impact of the illness was chiefly felt by the working classes.

The town's estimated population of 4,351 was divided into:

Gentry, professional men and their families	95
Tradesmen and their families	1,200
Mechanics, labourers and their families	3,061

The incidence of all deaths in the twelve months ending in October 1849 was classified as:

Gentry etc	2
Tradesmen etc	19
Artisans, labourers etc	254

The table showing the areas of the town in which cases of cholera were recorded reads:

Thorngate	154
Bridgegate	132
The Bank	37
Horse Market	22
(principally in two of the yards)	
Newgate	8
Galgate	8
Queen Street and Hall Street	5
Market Place	3

The inhabitants of the town presented a petition to the Board of Health in London which resulted in the visit of an official inspector, William Ranger Esq, who conducted an enquiry into conditions in the town with the help of some of the leading inhabitants whom he enlisted. He published a report (from which the above statistics are quoted) in which he examined the extent of the epidemic, enquired into its probable causes, and made suggestions for improving the town's housing and sanitary conditions.

Some of his findings were already well-known but the significance of the facts had not been realised. There was an inadequate water supply, consisting of only five public pumps and a slow-running spring on the Demesnes; other sources were private or shared wells, but a disturbing revelation was that the water supply was contaminated by sewage that had seeped into the earth, and that some wells had also been polluted by the decomposition of bodies in the churchyard which was situated on higher ground than the most densely populated part of the town. Some people had supplemented the water supply by collecting rain water from their roofs into butts, but it soon became putrid.

The drainage of the town was also very imperfect; the drains, designated as sewers, were really only surface drains and in some streets there were no drains at all. The deepest underground drains were only three feet (1m) below the surface, which meant that no cellars could be drained, and the largest surface sewer was the lower part of the castle's outer moat. All effluent that did not dry out on the surface flowed into the Tees.

Mr Ranger said that there were more than seventy overcrowded and ill-ventilated yards, and devoted a sixth of his report to giving detailed information on many of them. In Swinburnes Yard, he said, thirty-two people had lived in one house; nearly all of them contracted cholera and fifteen of them died. It was later discovered that other people had used the well in that yard. In all, forty-three people had used the well, and twenty-eight of them had died. The yard was a cul-de-sac and contained only one privy, for shared use. In Old Priory Yard there was only one privy for fifteen houses, with a large cesspool, surrounded by houses, and it was said that it had not been emptied 'for years'.

Some examples were outstandingly bad. Kirtleys Yard, on the Bank, had an uneven paved surface on which offal and stagnant water lay; in the yard there were pigstyes, a midden, and one privy; a cellar below a house had been converted into a cesspit which, when inspected, had a six inch (15cm) layer of sewage in it. People were living directly over the cellar, the floor of their room consisting of wooden boards with large holes in places, through which infectious and foul-smelling vapours passed into the room from the cellar.

Not only did such conditions have a vitiating effect on people's lives, but the overcrowded rooms shared by children and adults of both sexes and all ages prevented any of the ordinary privacy which most people would expect. This was worsened by the shortage of privies in many of the yards; in one example, five men, five women and three children all shared one privy without a cesspit, so that the excrement and urine was simply emptied onto the surface of the yard.

Such circumstances, said the report, led to people being 'destitute of the means of observing the ordinary rules of decency', and Mr Ranger incorporated in his report a section on the moral and spiritual aspects of life among these people. The Reverend Mr Dugard wrote this part of the report and said that in his two years as incumbent of the church he had found 'an exceedingly low tone' and 'an utter indifference and apathy to religion'. The adult population was almost beyond hope of amendment, he said, and the younger generation seemed doomed to a similar future.

He outlined the course of the degradation of young people, beginning with 'gambling schools' in secluded places where boys were instructed by experienced gamblers; then the young players adjourned to public houses where drinking and smoking became habitual; this, said Mr Dugard, 'further depraves the mind and brutalizes the desires, and in a year or two the animal passions become paramount'. At the age of fifteen or sixteen, boys and girls 'quit the parental roof and shamelessly cohabit together'. Mr Ranger was given a long list of unmarried couples, some of them having as many as eight illegitimate children.

The system of employment in the factories had much to answer for. At the age of twelve or thirteen, boys and girls received wages into their own hands, and as they grew older they earned more, until they felt they could become independent of their parents. The joint wages of two teenagers was not, however, sufficient to provide them with any accommodation better than a slum.

Too many adult workers were employed erratically in some of the carpet factories; when orders were plentiful, men were employed for sixteen-hour days or in twelve-hour shifts. When 'rush orders' had been fulfilled, the same men were unemployed for ten or so days at a time. This had a bad effect on their health, for during periods of unemployment they ate scantily and were unfit for working long hours in the days when work was plentiful again. Whilst unemployed, the men often turned to drink for recreation while they had money, and then some turned to crime to gain more money until they were again in work.

Barnard Castle's reputation for undesirable standards of behaviour, including sexual laxity and crime, can be confirmed from sources other than Mr Ranger's report. When the Teesdale Poor Law Union was formed in 1836, financial aid was given in respect of nearly 250 cases of illegitimacy, though it is only fair to add that the rate of illegitimacy was higher in the rural areas than in the town. The Union Workhouse itself was not free from blame, for in 1841 two female inmates gave birth to children that must have been conceived while they were resident in the workhouse in Galgate. In this case, strong suspicion put the blame on the master of the workhouse.

Crimes of drunkenness, illicit sex, profanity, assault, theft and manslaughter that were brought before the magistrates court in 1871 were committed more commonly in the lower end of the town than anywhere else in Barnard Castle. In 1851 Mr Justice Cresswell, speaking at Durham Assizes, referred to Barnard Castle as 'a sink of vice and profligacy'. One woman, by the 1860s, was reported to have been sent to prison for the one hundred and fifth time. In 1856 William Fordyce wrote in his history of County Durham that in recent years the County Bridge in Barnard Castle had 'acquired a sort of notoriety in consequence of murders and other outrages having been committed there'.

Mr Ranger's report was not primarily concerned with moral behaviour, but he tacitly, and correctly, assumed that people's behaviour was closely related to the conditions in which they lived. His recommendations were mainly concerned with the provision of proper sewers and drains, and a clean water supply. He recommended that all premises should be linked by drains to main sewers. A water supply should be laid on, fit for drinking, cooking and cleansing. All sewage should be conveyed well clear of the town. In every public yard there should be fire-points to provide water for cleansing yard and street surfaces, as well as for giving security against fires. Culs-de-sac should have a free flow of air. Slaughter houses and tan-yards should be away from human dwellings.

The most far-reaching reform was to be the creation, by election, of a Local Board of Health under the terms of the Public Health Act of 1848, to govern all questions of public health in the town and to provide necessary improvements by levying a town rate. Only property owners could vote at the election of the local board, and candidates had to be men of some substance, possessing, for instance, personal or real estate to the value of £600 and rated for poor relief at an annual value of at least £20. The first local board consisted of the Reverend George Dugard, who came top of the poll and was made chairman, three solicitors, two surgeons, two druggists, one physician, a currier, a farmer, and a carpet manufacturer. They appointed a clerk at £20 a year, and an inspector of nuisances at £7. Other appointments were a treasurer and an inspector of lodging houses, neither of whom was paid; the only other official was a rate collector who received no fixed salary but was given two pence for every pound which he collected.

The Barnard Castle Local Board of Health was only the third to be created in the country, and began its duties on the 27th July 1850.

IV

Recovery
1850–1900

The members and officials of the new Local Board of Health began their duties with zeal and decisiveness. Sewers were laid underground on the line of the main streets and the old Back Lane, and smaller drains were connected to them. In the spacious streets the procedure was straightforward, but the crowded areas at the lower end of the town presented more difficulties.

Nevertheless, seventy drains from Thorngate and Bridgegate were connected with main sewers which discharged into the Tees below the town, while other drains flowed into the river at any convenient point. Throughout the town nearly fifty inspection points were installed, and by 1856 over three miles (5km) of sewers had been laid. There were still many neglected areas, including a large part of Bridgegate which was not connected to a sewer at all, but the overall progress was remarkable.

The installation of a sewage system made an adequate water supply absolutely essential. The board appointed Mr Ranger as its consultant engineer, and his first task was to find a sufficient supply of soft water, the old wells and springs producing water that was considered too hard for either domestic or industrial use. Despite having earlier suggested a supply from Stainton Hill, Mr Ranger investigated the whole surrounding area and found what he wanted at Stony Keld in the parish of Bowes, about four and a half miles (7km) away. Water was conducted from there to an underground reservoir which was constructed on the Bowes to Barnard Castle road, near a farm called Westwood, and then conveyed to Barnard Castle, where in pipes, diminishing from seven to one and a half inches (18cm—4cm) in diameter, it was connected to individual houses or shared taps in yards. The board encouraged many residents to use the new supply to lime-wash their premises as a disinfectant, and to brighten up the houses and yards.

There was some opposition in Barnard Castle, as in other parts of the country, to these measures. Owners of insanitary properties had always been reluctant to spend money on improvements, and objected to being told what to do by either a national or local board of health. Many people saw the 1848 Public Health Act as the ominous beginnings of state interference into personal matters. However, in his first annual report the chairman of the local board said that even the strongest opposition had been diminished by a few months' experience of the benefits of a pure and abundant water supply. For some people the laying of water pipes had been frightening, for it disturbed them to see their streets being dug up, and when, as occasionally happened, a pipe burst and water shot into the air they were further alarmed. Eventually their fears were dispelled by the successful completion of the undertaking.

The chairman felt that if any error had been made it was that the board had proceeded with 'a too rigid economy'. In 1854 the Westwood reservoir was found to

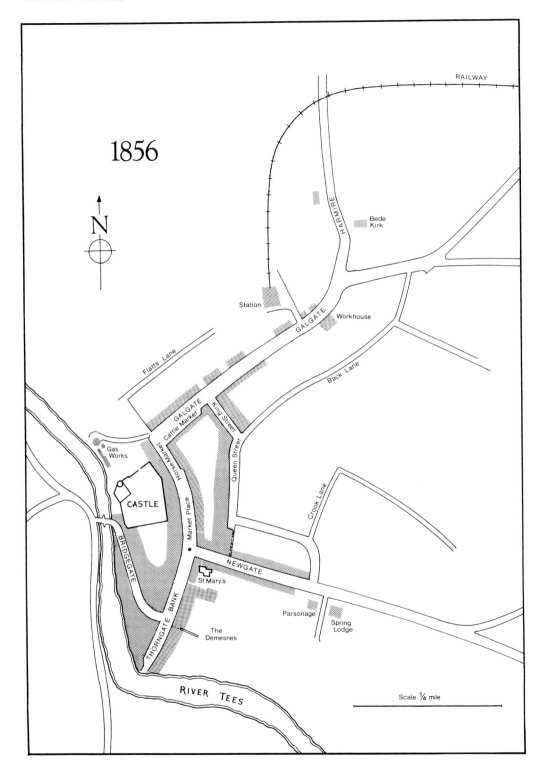

be inadequate, and work began on a larger one farther up the Bowes road, so in this respect alone the chairman was right in saying that the board had carried economy too far.

Some recommendations of the 1850 report were delayed. Untreated sewage flowed directly into the Tees for the next forty years though, as time passed, arrangements were made for sewers to discharge their contents farther downstream from the town. The churchyard continued to be used for burials until 1865 when a new cemetery with a mortuary chapel was opened beside the Back Lane. The cemetery's drainage system flowed through underground pipes until it, too, discharged its effluent into the river.

Another defect of the town was not remedied at all. No action was taken to increase the ventilation of the streets and yards. The mill and the factory at the end of Thorngate left only a narrow gap opening onto the river, and the Market Cross filled most of the width of the road at the top of the Bank, while the yards remained as airless as when the cholera infected them.

The lower end of the town was also facing a new threat, as the fear of unemployment loomed over the employees of the carpet factories. The demand for Barnard Castle carpets had begun to diminish. As early as 1832 some of the town's leading carpet manufacturers had stressed the need for the railway to come to Barnard Castle, for it was already clear that the days of horse-drawn wagons were numbered. Barnard Castle was becoming isolated, and buyers preferred to deal with firms which were situated within easy reach of other towns with similar industries, so that they might find in one neighbouring town what they failed to find in another. Moreover, after 1849, Barnard Castle became feared as a 'cholera town', and another, unexpected, blow to the trade was the invention of linoleum which was patented in 1860 and 1863, and became a cheaper alternative to Barnard Castle's reversible form of carpeting. The decline in the carpet trade was gradual rather than dramatic, but in 1870 Monkhouse and Whitfield's works closed, having once employed 200 men, and well before the end of the century no working carpet factories remained in the town. Throughout the years of industrial decline, many people suffered poverty and some left the town to seek employment elsewhere, including the Colonies and America. Even before the final closure of the factories, the population fell from 4,608 in 1851 to 4,269 in 1881.

Meanwhile, after very prolonged negotiations, the railway had come to Barnard Castle. Many public meetings were held before this was achieved; when strong enough support had been demonstrated, the Darlington and Stockton Railway Company was asked to sponsor a line, but strong objections were expressed by the duke of Cleveland as he did not want the railway to pass through his estates of Raby Castle or Selaby Hall. Eventually a public company was formed, and the duke agreed to the line crossing his farmland so long as it did not enter his parkland. Parliament gave its approval in April 1854 to a line linking Darlington and Barnard Castle, and the queen gave her royal assent in July.

After all the delay and frustration, work on the line proceeded rapidly and it was completed within two years. A dignified and ornamental passenger station was built behind the north side of Galgate. After this line had been opened, other lines followed more easily. An important link with the west of the country was formed by opening a line across Stainmore in 1861. This made it necessary to alter the location of Barnard Castle's station, which was no longer a terminus. The station near Galgate became a goods station, and a new passenger station was built about a third of a mile (0.5km) north of the old one. Cattle pens and coal staithes were erected alongside the Station

Barnard Castle's second passenger station.

Trains ready to depart for Darlington (on the left) and Bishop Auckland.

The main platform.

Road which linked the two stations. The impressive portico at the entrance to the old passenger station was acquired by the town of Saltburn, where it was erected in the Valley Gardens as a memorial to Prince Albert, who died in 1861.

In 1863 a line to Bishop Auckland was opened, speeding the delivery of coal from the Durham coalfield to Barnard Castle, and in 1868 a new line had its terminus at Middleton-in-Teesdale and became valuable in encouraging tourists to visit the beauties of the upper dale.

In a wide variety of ways the railway constantly asserted itself as an element in the development of the town over the next 100 years. It caused the creation of whole streets of new houses, some for employees of the railway itself, and some to accommodate the increasing flow of visitors to the town; the style of the town's architecture changed as building materials were brought from distant parts of Britain. Blue slate and brick replaced local stone when some new houses were built, but other contractors stayed faithful to the traditional materials; the railways, even then, had a part to play, for some men who worked in Teesdale's quarries travelled to and from work by train. Other commuters worked in Darlington and Bishop Auckland in shops and offices.

The achievement of bringing a railway to Barnard Castle was seen as a fine example of what could be done by a spirited public effort on behalf of the town. Mr John Longbottom, a pioneer of the Barnard Castle Co-operative Society, seized upon this point when he urged the town to have its own co-operative shop. 'Co-operation is',

The portico of Barnard Castle's first passenger station, removed to Saltburn.

The Bowes Museum.

The North Eastern County School, now Barnard Castle School.

One of the Co-operative Society's flourishing shops in Bridgegate.

he said, 'the great question of the day ... We have in this town co-operative gas companies and co-operative railway companies, and, lastly, co-operative woollen companies.' He acknowledged that other businessmen would see the movement as an enemy of private enterprise, but despite opposition from other shop-keepers, a 'co-op' was established in the town, at first in a private house, and then in a small shop in Bridgegate, until in 1878 it was able to buy extensive premises on both sides of the narrow street, with warehouses from which goods were delivered in the society's own horse-drawn vehicles. The society clearly fulfilled a need in the poorer and most neglected part of the town.

In 1877 two holidaymakers who toured Teesdale published a book on their experiences and referred to Bridgegate as 'one of the back slums of the town', and noted 'passages round which are congregated knots of idle, slatternly women'. There were still other areas of the town where conditions were far from satisfactory with, for example, too many people sharing one lavatory in Hall Street, and an offensive slaughter-house existing too near dwellings on the Bank and affecting children at the Wesleyan school. The National Board of Health was still sending reminders to the local board to check for any cases of cholera, and the water supply was examined and found to be pure — or, at least, it contained no sewage. However, some holidaymakers left the town when the water from the reservoir tasted stagnant, and when Messrs William Smith and Sons, who made machinery for cleansing and watering roads, gave a public demonstration of one of their appliances which was meant to spray water over about twenty feet (6m) of road, no water emerged. On examination, it was found that the holes of the distributor were blocked by living organisms which had been in the water mains. Some of the creatures were half an inch (1cm) long and had to be pulled out of the holes in which they had become wedged.

William Smith and Sons was the biggest of the industries that were established in the Back Lane. Their premises were on the side of the road that was open countryside, so they had room to expand as they prospered. As pioneers in creating municipal machinery for cleaning roads and laying the dust in streets, they found markets in Britain, and parts of Europe and Asia. It was a remarkable achievement for a firm whose origins had been a blacksmith's shop in a market town.

The area around the Back Lane continued to become built up. By 1862 it had firmly become the town's second industrial area, and included another foundry owned by a member of the Smith family, William Smith junior. Other buildings sprang up: the police station moved from Bridgegate to the junction of Hall Street and George Street, and then in 1861 to Queen Street; in 1868 a Roman Catholic school was built next to it. A brass and iron foundry opened behind the south side of Newgate, and there was talk of turning the Hole in the Wall into a proper road to link Newgate directly to the Back Lane, but nothing came of it; and the post office moved from Newgate to the town centre, since the railway now brought the mail which had formerly come by road over the Abbey Bridge after being collected from the mail coach at Greta Bridge.

A new vicarage, called the Parsonage, had been built beside Demesnes Lane opposite Spring Lodge, and the former parsonage at the corner of the Back Lane and Newgate was partly rebuilt as Spring Grove, a private residence which also catered for visitors. In the enclosed fields which lay beyond, an astonishing transformation was about to take place. Thirteen of the fields, and a market garden, were turned into a park with formal and informal gardens, and a massive museum was built in the style of a French town hall or chateau. This was the Bowes Museum, created by John Bowes of Streatlam Castle, son of the tenth earl, and his wife, Josephine Benoîte, countess of Montalbo. Both John and Josephine Bowes were keen collectors of works of art, and they decided to increase the pace at which they were acquiring new items and to put them on display for the benefit of the public. A plateau was created in the fields, and on it Mrs Bowes laid the foundation stone of a magnificent museum in 1869. The building itself progressed slowly, for though there were sometimes as many as 100 men working on it under the direction of a local building contractor, Mr Joseph Kyle, stone was not quarried and delivered as quickly as had been expected. It was January 1874 before the roof timbers were in place, and a fortnight later Mrs Bowes was dead. Her grief-stricken husband travelled in Europe, and work on the museum proceeded fitfully.

Local people maintained a lively interest in the project and excitement grew as display cases and exhibits began to arrive, even though the building was unfinished. Ten years passed and Mr Bowes himself was in failing health. He died on 9th October 1885. Barnard Castle was in mourning. Neither of the founders had lived to see the dream become reality. Progress again was delayed, as Mr Bowes' affairs were in a complicated state, but a committee of management kept arrangements going. At last the museum was opened to the public on 10th June 1892, amid great rejoicing. The town was decorated with flags, and large scrolls bearing messages of congratulation were hung in the streets; individual houses were decked with leafy branches and flowers, and the railway station was beautified with banks of ferns and other greenery. A grand procession consisting of members of the town's sporting, social, and official organisations led by the band of the 3rd Battalion Durham Light Infantry, marched through the town to the formal opening by Sir Joseph Pease MP.

During the protracted arrangements for creating the Bowes Museum, another great enterprise had been proceeding much more quickly in the fields to the east of the museum park. This was the creation of the North Eastern County School, one of a series of schools that had been opened in various places in England to provide public school-style education in a manner affordable to middle-class parents. In 1869, with the encouragement of Durham University, a committee began to look for funds and was approached by two sets of trustees. One represented the estate of the late Benjamin Flounders, a businessman from Yarm who had left money to be used in education; the second group represented St John's Hospital, in Newgate, still aiming to found the grammar school for Barnard Castle as they had been instructed by the Charity Commissioners in 1863. The hospital could contribute £10,710 to the new scheme, the Flounders Trust could provide £31,495, and the commissioners gave their approval provided that £10,000 was raised by public subscription. This was achieved, mainly by donations from residents of the three north-eastern counties, Northumberland, Durham and the North Riding of Yorkshire.

The building rose with the speed that characterised the whole proceedings. Under the control of Joseph Kyle, fresh from his experience as contractor for the Bowes Museum, a workforce of up to 200 men had completed the building by January 1886. There was an open day, on which a steady stream of local people passed through the buildings for several hours, and a fortnight later 116 boarders and 12 day boys entered the school as pupils.

Thus Newgate, instead of ending abruptly on the edge of the countryside, led to two of the town's most outstanding buildings, one in the French style and the other in the English neo-Jacobean tradition, standing prominently on the slopes of Teesdale.

On the western boundary of the museum park, another unusual block of buildings had risen in 1864. This was the headquarters of the 3rd Battalion of the Durham

Prominent nineteenth century buildings in the eastern part of the town: the barracks, the Bowes Museum, and the North Eastern County School. In the foreground, left, is the Primitive Methodist Church, built in 1887.

Light Infantry, formerly the 1st South Durham Militia; in front of the main buildings was a parade ground, approached through a castellated archway, with stone doorways on each side, in which sentries stood. There were also annual military camps under canvas on the big field, known as the Camp Field, across the river at Decrbolt; there were officers' camps beside the Westwick road, and sometimes drill parades took place, to the accompaniment of a military band, on the Demesnes.

The barracks, the County School and the Bowes Museum all added new aspects to the life of Barnard Castle, bringing not only trade but also cultural, social and educational benefits to what had been rather an insular community.

Much of this was due to the coming of the railway, thirty years earlier, without which, for example, the school could not have operated, for the railway was needed to transport an increasing number of boarders to and from the north-eastern counties three times a year. Members of the Durham Light Infantry similarly needed transport,

The cattle market in lower Galgate, before improvements began in 1873.

Smartly-dressed farmers and young onlookers pose with sheep near the drinking fountain in the cattle market.

Cattle and farm-workers on their way from the market pause between two of the Galgate enclosures.

when so many of the men attending the annual camps came from Sunderland and Hartlepool, and the added attraction of a grand museum and park brought increasing numbers of tourists to Barnard Castle.

The railway also caused an embarrassment, however: because of the passenger station's situation, all the visitors who came to Barnard Castle gained their first impression of the town from Galgate — and Galgate was not, in the 1860s, an attractive street. Upper Galgate led to lower Galgate, which was still the cattle market. As a country road the street was possibly acceptable, but not as an introduction to a town that had pretensions to be a holiday resort. The chairman of the Board of Health, Mr W Watson, called it an 'eyesore' and an 'unsightly place'. Only the central part of the road had a firm surface in lower Galgate, and loose soil washed down onto it from the higher side, while in places it became boggy in wet weather. The other side of the road was treated as wasteland; boys played informal cricket on it and a travelling theatre company erected its tent outside the Three Horse Shoes.

The higher side of upper Galgate was also a waste space, so little used that on one occasion a man scythed a crop of hay from it. At other times an agricultural dealer and a cartwright displayed their wares on it, rocks and unwanted gateposts lay about on it, and the children of one family were said to be 'committing nuisances of the most objectionable kind' on it.

The Board of Health began its improvement scheme in lower Galgate. In 1873 members accepted a scheme to erect, at public expense, an ornamental drinking fountain for both man and beast. They planted an avenue of trees through which the central road ran, and then they turned their attention to upper Galgate. They created four areas of grass and shrubs on the wasteland that bordered the road, and to prevent the unseemly use of them, these areas were surrounded by iron railings, leaving space for a minor road along the upper side of the grass. The clerk firmly warned the board that these railed enclosures were illegal because they were permanent obstructions on a public highway but, undeterred, the board proceeded with its plans and planted sycamore trees in the enclosures, forming a continuous line of trees down upper Galgate in the early 1890s.

People still complained about cattle straying onto the pavements and leaving them in an unfit state for pedestrians, especially in lower Galgate. It was clear that it was time the cattle market moved elsewhere, so in 1892 purpose-built accommodation was made in Flatts Lane. An octagonal auction building, connected to one long shed with over seventy open pens behind it, was created. For a time, the bottom end of Galgate was still referred to as the cattle market, with the new arrangements being called the Auction Mart.

As Galgate became a more acceptable thoroughfare, new streets began to branch off it. Station Road was built up for part of its length on the side opposite the goods yard and terminated at its northern end at a farmhouse which faced the passenger station, five fields away. Baliol Street was the first street to be built adjoining Galgate, and it was followed by Marshall Street, probably the first street in the town to be built with bricks. Finally, John Street was built opposite Station Road.

All these streets were built piecemeal, with new houses being added from time to time. Marshall Street was begun in 1873 and was not completed for at least four years, and when houses were built on the middle part of the Back Lane, five were built in a row called Headlam Gardens and then seven more called Headlam Terrace were added; more houses, opposite the new cemetery, formed South View; and the farthest row was called Victoria Terrace as a compliment to the queen on her diamond jubilee.

A view of upper Galgate, where the new enclosures are well established. A trial area of macadam has been laid at the right-hand side, adjacent to a road crossing composed of rectangular stone blocks.

Outside the town, Prospect Place was built by 1868 on the edge of a former quarry, and more houses in an isolated site were built to form three sides of a rectangle, known respectively as Bede Terrace, Bede Terrace West and Bede Terrace North — now known as part of Bede Road and Kirk View. The names came from the Bede Kirk, a church dating from the twelfth century, though later altered to a farm, which stood in a field nearby. Some of this development was built by Joseph Kyle, who was also responsible for the line of houses on the south-east side of Galgate, which had the effect of giving the street a much more urban appearance. By 1883 almost the whole of the town's main street was built up.

In the early stages of this development, while space was still available, rich men began to build large houses in extensive grounds in the upper part of the town. One called Beaconsfield House led the way. It had a square, uncompromising appearance, though ornamental iron pinnacles gave a flourish to the roof-line; the house had a large conservatory and gardens laid out in formal walks and lined with trees. At the other end of John Street was, unusually, a brick-built spacious residence belonging to Robert Taylor Richardson. It had two vineries, for early and late crops, and its grounds extended across the Back Lane to include a copse and fields. The house is now the central part of the Richardson Hospital, but was originally named the Starlings. John Smith, of William Smith and Sons, built a stone house with entries to the grounds from both Galgate and the Back Lane; it had a billiard room in the house and a

The original auction ring at the purpose-built cattle market in Flatts Lane, now Vere Road.

tennis court in the grounds. It was called Grove Park, and when the foundation stone was laid by Mrs Wilson, wife of the builder, the occasion was said to be commemorative of the Victorian era because it showed how an individual craftsman could become the employer of a workforce, and rise in society. The initials of John Smith and his wife were ornamentally carved over the front door.

The town was growing fast, and was looking prosperous. Its population was rising more slowly, but by the end of the century totalled 4,594. Again, it was the railway which was largely responsible. Its own staff made a considerable addition to the town's residents: there was a station master, his assistant, a booking clerk, two parcel clerks, a telegraph clerk, North Eastern railway police, a ticket collector, two guards, six general porters, a parcel porter, a locomotive inspector, two engine drivers, a goods manager and a 'permanent way' inspector. They had a strong sense of unity, and formed a branch of the

The front door of Grove Park, described as 'commemorative of the Victorian era'.

Amalgamated Society of Railway Servants; at Christmas 1891 they decorated the station and treated themselves on Christmas Eve to a knife and fork tea at Morton's Cocoa Rooms, near the Market Cross, where they enjoyed songs, recitations and readings.

The County School's numbers rose to 300 boarders and 19 day boys, which also led to an increase in employment in the town, and the arrival of hundreds of holidaymakers enlivened trade and created more, albeit seasonal, jobs. Shops broadened their range of goods, and the local newspaper the *Teesdale Mercury* (founded in 1854) began to include lists of the names of visitors to the town and the addresses at which they stayed. Not every visitor was mentioned, but in some years as many as 200 families, couples or single visitors were recorded in one week in

Morton's Restaurant, near the Market Cross, where the railwaymen held their Christmas party.

August. The new villas and streets in bright unstained sandstone with gardens in front of them, and the green enclosures in Galgate, all combined to give the town an air of elegance which appealed to the holidaymaker.

One building which made an impressive impact was the new Wesleyan church which was completed in 1894 at the lower end of the avenue of trees in Galgate. It stood on a site previously occupied by two small houses, and the contrast between them and the new lofty building in its conspicuous position was symptomatic of the changing face of the town. When the Wesleyans moved from the Bank to Galgate, the Primitive Methodists had already moved from the Bank to Newgate seven years earlier, and built a new church near the entrance to the Hole in the Wall. It was all part of the trend to erect public buildings and private houses in the upper, more salubrious, part of the town.

The two houses at the end of lower Galgate that were demolished to make way for the new Methodist Church.

Lower Galgate at the end of the nineteenth century; the Methodist Church (1894) provides a focal point at the end of the avenue, and a horse finds refreshment at the drinking fountain of 1874.

Joseph Kyle's row of houses in Galgate gave an urban tone to what had been a rural approach to the town.

Mr Richardson's residence, the Starlings, after it was enlarged to create the Richardson Hospital.

By the time these two Methodist churches were built, the parish church had been rescued from its decaying condition. The disturbed, uneven floor was re-laid, the heavy galleries were removed, new windows were inserted into the south wall of the chancel, and the south door, which had long been disused and plastered over, was re-opened, thus restoring one of the oldest features of the church. All these improvements were achieved within two years, and the building was officially re-opened by the bishop of Durham on the 8th December 1870. Three years later the old tower, which had been found to be unsafe, was demolished and replaced in 1874 by a new tower eighty feet (24m) high, in which a chiming clock was installed, the gift of Mr William Watson of Spring Lodge. The church bells had been silent since 1868 when the poor condition of the tower was first noticed, and the re-hanging of the bells was sufficiently important to inspire a poem by the Reverend Blackburn Clarke, a native of the town; it included the lines:

The Primitive Methodist Church (1887) in Newgate photographed shortly before its demolition in 1992.

Ring out a peal as in days that are olden,
Ring out a peal with the vigour of yore,
Tell us your notes are yet silvern and golden,
Tell us ye still have sweet music in store'.

During the restoration of St Mary's Church, a new nonconformist church was built in Newgate where the parish hall now stands. It was a Unitarian, or Free Christian, church and its spire gave a new appearance to the street's skyline. The biggest single change to the traditional appearance of the town, however, was the building of Backhouses Bank in 1878 which brought a startling modern note into the Market Place, for less ornate buildings, including the Queens Head, had to be demolished to make way for it. The conversion of other buildings into shops became a frequent occurrence and many were ornamented with decorative cast-iron strips above their windows. These lingered as a feature of the town for about 100 years, but when they rusted they were not replaced.

An increased number of shops, more than seventy boarding houses, and a new steam laundry (which must have been a boon to landladies) all suggest a busy town,

St Mary's Parish Church: *(above)* before restoration; *(below)* after restoration and the addition of the new tower.

(Above) the Market Place before 1878; and *(below)* after Backhouses Bank brought a change of architectural style.

but the summer season was short and during the rest of the year there were quiet days. Two tourists, describing the town in 1894, called it a 'thriving but somewhat sleepy place', and wrote: 'The little town except on a market day is as quiet a long street of dull grey houses as can be met with.'

Market day was an event in itself. Though for a while the cattle market was held only fortnightly, the corn market grew in significance, and Barnard Castle became one of the towns which was used by the Board of Trade to calculate the average price of corn throughout the country. The Butter Market became uncomfortably crowded, and glazed wooden panels were placed between the outer pillars of the building to shelter the women who sat near the edge of the arcade. (The town's fire engine was moved from the church and kept in the central part of the ground floor of the Butter Market.) The farmers and their wives travelled to market in small horse-drawn vehicles called tub-traps. While the traps were parked in the street, the horses were in stables situated along the yards running at

Decorative ironwork over the door and window gives distinction to this shop in the Horse Market.

right angles to the street. Most of the stables belonged to the twenty-six inns in the town, and it was said that 1,000 horses could be accommodated in one day.

Market day was a real social occasion, and was also much enjoyed by tourists. One of them, J E Buckrose, who was rambling through the northern dales, recorded his impressions in a book which was published in 1913. He recalls that he arrived by train and walked down:

> ... a long road reaching to a large Market Place. It was a market day and the fine open space was filled with carts and old-fashioned gigs and vehicles of all kinds,

Some of Barnard Castle's yards: *(clockwise from top left)* Waterloo Yard, Raby Yard, Star Yard and Sayers Yard. The first three were attached to inns, and the fourth leads to private houses.

Market day: *(above)* the stallholders and customers arrive in the morning; *(below)* by noon it is a hive of activity.

A quiet day in the Horse Market.

while the streets were thronged with fresh-complexioned farmers and farmers' wives and daughters, who greeted each other on the pavement with the jolly friendliness of those who live in remote places, and find in 'market-day' what some people look for in a London season.

There were young men in their best clothes making sheepish remarks to flower-faced girls in coats and skirts of every colour in the rainbow — older men joked with capable farmers' wives who possessed, nearly all of them, the fine dignity which comes from having a place in the world and filling it well and through all other sounds came the constant chorus of the weather which enters into every conversation, and no wonder, for on that the prosperity of the whole dale depends.

Within the town's own social sphere, the formation of clubs and societies became almost commonplace, generally catering for the more affluent classes. There was a horticultural society with an annual flower show in the grounds of Spring Lodge; the Teesdale Rifle Volunteers shared an open-air range in Deepdale with the 2nd Volunteer Battalion of the DLI; the Barnard Lodge of Freemasons was founded in 1869 and had its own premises in Newgate by 1878; there was a Conservative club, a Conservative Working-men's Club, and a Junior Liberal Club; an agricultural club and a branch of the Farmers Protection Association served one aspect of the town's trade, while the other was represented by the Industrial Society.

The town cricket club had moved from Woolhouse to the Baliol Street ground in 1863 but was rather exclusive, requiring a subscription and proper clothing, and its playing members had to pay for rail travel for away games and sometimes for a dinner at the Kings Head after its home fixtures. The golf club, having begun at Wyse Hill in the parish of Startforth in 1892, also moved to the northern outskirts of Barnard Castle, where at first it had a nine-hole course with a par score of forty.

Association football was very strong in the town with, in 1887, the main team playing on the cricket field in winter and, ten years later, having its own ground at Nab End which was soon to become a building site for Raby Avenue. There were at least four other football teams in the town, some playing midweek games so that shop assistants could play on half-closing days. A Barnard Castle man, Robert ('Bob') Chatt, played for Aston Villa, and in the cup final of 1895 against West Bromwich Albion, on the Crystal Palace ground, he scored the only goal of the match. His fellow townsman, Jimmy Welford, was also playing for Aston Villa that day; he had the extraordinary distinction of playing in the cup finals of three different countries, England, Scotland and Ireland. Mr Chatt sometimes turned out for the Barnard Castle team and was a great attraction for spectators.

It was athletic sports meetings, however, which had, indirectly, the biggest impact on the history of the town. They were held once a year on the cricket field, and in 1885 a group of cyclists came to Barnard Castle at Whitsuntide weekend and attended the event. They were impressed by the town, its surroundings, the cycling and foot races on the cricket field, and the grand ball that was held in the evening. They spread the fame of the occasion, and in 1886 Barnard Castle became the venue for the annual North-Eastern Cyclists' Meet. The enthusiasm was tremendous: clubs cycled from Newcastle-upon-Tyne and were met at the top of the town by crowds bearing ornamental lanterns to conduct the cyclists through the darkening streets. Special trains were organised for other spectators and participants. In 1893, 5,000 people arrived by train, and 6,000 watched the sports. A great tradition had become firmly established as an occasion for jollity, serious athletic pursuits and, of course, economic benefit to the town.

Part of the second National school, showing a portion of the covered playground.

In an age that was also dedicated to education, the mechanics institute continued its good work, though it increasingly acquired a middle-class aura, but the most spectacular addition to the town's educational facilities was the building of a new National school which opened in 1892. It stood on the same site as its predecessor but was very much bigger and grander, being built with full regard to

Egglestone Abbey, two miles (3km) from Barnard Castle, a venue for school outings and day trips.
Reproduced from an old picture postcard.

The new aqueduct, known as the Water Bridge, gave pedestrians a fine view of the castle.

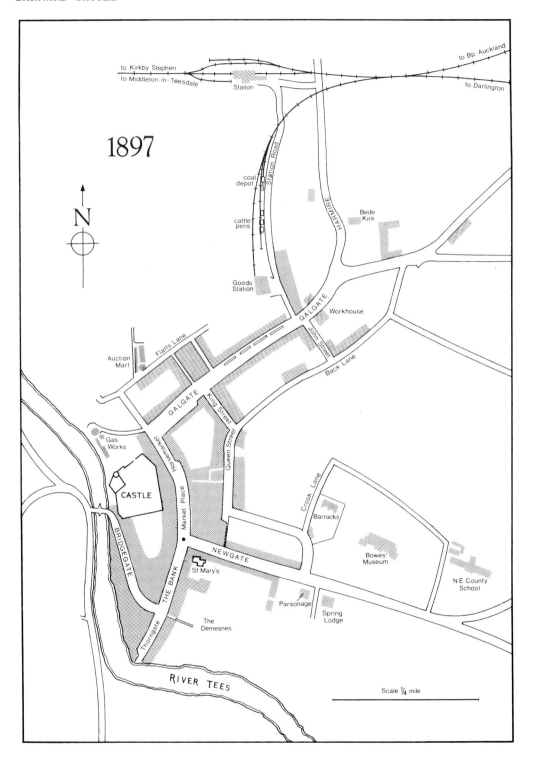

1897

N

to Kirkby Stephen
to Middleton-in-Teesdale
to Bp. Auckland
to Darlington

Station

coal depot

Station Road

HARMIRE

Bede Kirk

cattle pens

Goods Station

GALGATE

Workhouse

John Street

Back Lane

Flatts Lane

Auction Mart

GALGATE

King Street

Gas Works

Queen Street

Crook Lane

CASTLE

Horsemarket

Barracks

Bowes' Museum

Market Place

The Bank

NEWGATE

N.E. County School

BRIDGEGATE

St Mary's

Parsonage

Spring Lodge

Thorngate

The Demesnes

RIVER TEES

Scale ¼ mile

ventilation and lighting in the classrooms, and having a playground with a covered section for use in inclement weather. The cost of this school was largely defrayed by Mr William J Watson of Thorngate House and Spring Lodge, the son of the donor of the town clock and other benefactions.

The town was now well equipped with schools. In addition to the National and Wesleyan schools and the County School, there were several private schools of varying sizes and pretensions. Nevertheless, absenteeism from the National and Wesleyan schools caused concern, though it must be admitted that even official days of absence were remarkably frequent. The schools were closed, for example, for the annual flower show, a school 'treat' to Egglestone Abbey, the opening of the Bowes Museum, the opening of the Wesleyan chapel, a general election, and for half a day when a circus came to town. The Wesleyan authorities would not have closed the school for Hirings Day but, according to the log book, were 'forced' to do so by country children who would not have attended, anyway.

Bad behaviour was another cause for concern. Boys were seriously injured in the playground; seats in Flatts Woods were vandalised (a recurrent problem) in 1884; the flag pole which carried a warning when Deepdale shooting range was in use was broken in 1885; and in 1887 windows were smashed and a sixteen year old youth was sent to prison for fourteen days for setting fire to a haystack. In 1896 the *Teesdale Mercury* reported: 'A good deal of vandalism has recently been committed by the precocious youth of the town'.

The instances included damage to the Thorngate footbridge. This bridge was the second one on that site to replace the stepping-stones which had served as a river-crossing until the first bridge was built in 1871. Unwisely, the design of the first bridge depended on two pillars standing in midstream. In March 1881 there was a severe flood when a heavy fall of snow was followed by a quick thaw and torrential rain. The swollen River Tees crashed against the pillars with such force that one of them became unstable and the whole structure fell into the raging water, drowning two men who were standing on the bridge at the time. The new bridge was completed about three years later.

In 1893 an aqueduct, generally known as the 'Water Bridge', was built across the Tees, upstream of the castle. It was created by the Stockton and Middlesbrough (later the Tees Valley) Water Board to convey water to the growing towns by the Tees some thirty miles (50km) away. The water came from reservoirs that had been constructed on the River Lune and River Balder, tributaries of the Tees above Barnard Castle. The water board allowed the public to use the aqueduct as a footbridge, which added another charm to the developing town. It was immediately popular, and hundreds of people enjoyed the new view of the castle and its cliff, reflected in the still water above the weir of Ullathornes Mill. The aqueduct, together with the Thorngate footbridge and the more ancient Abbey Bridge and the County Bridge, offered visitors and residents the opportunity for a variety of 'round' walks from which to enjoy beautiful river scenery.

Such walks added to the pleasure given by the appearance of the new houses, the tree-lined streets, the Galgate enclosures and the new churches. As visitors strolled towards the historic Market Place or the modern Bowes Museum, they did not see the less salubrious areas in which some of the town's residents lived. It was from this limited viewpoint that the author of a Durham County Directory wrote: 'During the summer months when its trees and gardens attached to the houses are in leaf and flower, Barnard Castle as a country town has few equals.'

V

Modern Times
1900 to the Present Day

Barnard Castle's popularity as a tourist resort encouraged the local authorities to improve some of the town's least attractive features. The ravine beside the castle had been used as a rubbish dump for so long that it had become level with the foot of the castle wall. The Raby Estates water bailiff and gamekeeper, who lived nearby, protested: 'It is not good for tourists to see old boots, clogs, broken pottery, bottles, dead dogs, and filth in that place.' Attempts were made to stop people from continuing to leave refuse there, and the area became covered in rough grass, but old habits die hard and notices were erected telling people not to throw rubbish into the river instead.

The Urban District Council replaced the old Board of Health in 1894, and a year later the town's first sewage works were built. By 1913 the difficult problem of disposing of sewage from the overcrowded houses of Bridgegate was solved by laying an external sewer elevated on a line of masonry pillars of decreasing height running along the riverbank. Lavatory outlets were linked to this large black pipe, which conveyed its

A view of the Tees as it flowed past Bridgegate. The new sewer, provided in 1913, can be seen on the right. This is a hand-coloured card and not all the colours are accurate.

A band concert in the Bowes Museum Park.

contents into the sewage system to the east of the town. In the same year the town's first public lavatories were built underground in the Market Place, despite considerable opposition.

Meanwhile the town's recreational facilities also increased. The Bowes Museum Park was maturing, and in 1908 a first-class bowling green was added to its attractions, followed in 1912 by a bandstand which replaced an ornamental pool that had been at first a centrepiece of the formal garden. This was an instant success, and special trains brought people to band concerts on Wednesday evenings in the summer.

The cricket club, which employed a professional player-groundsman, was still regarded as beyond the means of the working classes. The football club became Barnard Castle Athletic in 1921, and moved to the Ten Fields ground on the eastern edge of the town where its opening match, against Witton Park, was watched by 1,500 spectators. The golf club had still only nine holes, but by 1913 the record for playing eighteen holes (twice round) was 79. In 1920, when Sunday play was introduced, sixteen local clergymen wrote in protest.

Flatts Woods were so important as an attraction that their various pathways were given names: the Cleveland Walk ran from Nab End, at the western end of Raby Avenue, through the woods towards the Red Well; the path which linked the Cleveland Walk to the mouth of Percy Beck was the King's Walk; the path upstream by the Tees was called the Ladies' Walk, but farther on, where it became rough and undulating, it was called the Rock Walk because it led to rocky cliffs about a mile and a half (2km) from the town. The grassy area at the junction of the Tees and Percy Beck was called the Bandstand or Bandfield because the town band or the band of the 3rd Battalion

Popular walks in the woods: *(above)* part of the Cleveland Walk, about 1900; *(right)* the steps on the Rock Walk, 1914; *(below)* another part of the Cleveland Walk, 1929.

The grassy area where the band played, at the junction of Percy Beck and the River Tees.

Durham Light Infantry sometimes played there on Sunday afternoons. Bathing was popular in a deep pool nearby, despite a warning sign erected on the advice of the coroner after a member of the DLI special reserves had drowned there in 1913. The number of anglers increased tenfold during the fifty years leading up to the Great War; the trout varied in size and the salmon varied in number, and the Tees was classed as a salmon river but not of the highest class.

People who wanted to explore Teesdale were well catered for. Guidebooks suggested over thirty excursions, for which bicycles, horses, ponies and traps or, as time passed, motor cars could be hired. The North Eastern Railway issued touring tickets enabling walkers or cyclists to alight at any station in Teesdale and rejoin the line at that or any another station. From Middleton-in-Teesdale station a horse-drawn wagonette took visitors to see High Force. For

High Force in flood; a popular excursion spot.

Decorated temporary headquarters of cycling clubs in the Market Place in 1909.

more energetic people, Barnard Castle's two cycling clubs, the Teesdale Wanderers and the Excelsior, welcomed visitors on their outings.

The annual Cyclists' Meet was so popular that it was described as the 'Premier Cyclists' Meet of the World'. Clubs whose members stayed the whole weekend in the town established temporary headquarters in various hotels, and decorated the outside of the buildings in elaborate and imaginative ways. The streets were hung with flags, and many new activities were added to the weekend's attractions. A fancy-dress procession through the town became a regular feature, watched by 25,000 people in 1904, and there were plays, dances, speech-making contests, visits to Rokeby, and cycle, running and walking races which attracted large crowds. Indoor events took place in the music hall that had been erected behind the Witham Testimonial in 1860.

The town's other building for public functions was the Victoria Hall, in a wide yard linking Newgate and Birch Road. It was a real Victorian theatre with a balcony and, at floor level, seating which could be removed for banquets and balls. Barnard Castle Operatic Society, formally founded in 1911, annually performed there and provided one of the highlights of the year, with special trains bringing audiences from the surrounding area. The town's first cinema opened in the former Wesleyan chapel in Wycliffe Yard, off the Bank, and advertised in a guidebook of 1913 as the Wycliffe Electric Picture Hall; and a travelling theatre sometimes visited the field opposite the Victoria Hall.

Farther along Birch Road a drill hall was erected near the barracks in 1913, and in July 1914 the 4th Battalion Durham Light Infantry provided an impressive spectacle when they 'laid up' their old colours in the parish church. Wearing full dress uniforms of red and green, and accompanied by their bugle band, the soldiers paraded their old and new colours in Galgate, watched by a large crowd, some of whom used as a tiered vantage point the three-stepped curb which the Urban District Council had added in 1912 on the higher side of the street. It was all part of a colourful era.

Sixteen days later, however, war broke out. It was not unexpected. Twelve troop trains had passed through Barnard Castle Station on one Sunday in June, and notices had been publicly posted giving orders to the Territorial Army. On the first Sunday of war, a packed congregation heard the vicar's opinion that Britain's entry into the war showed that the country was godly at heart. 'What else could we have done?', he asked. In the Witham Hall a public meeting was convened to ask: 'What can we do now?' A distress fund was founded to relieve any local suffering caused by the war, and another organisation was established to send comforts to local men away on active service. The Urban District Council formed a war emergency committee and a local defence corps was mustered, first in civilian dress and later in uniform. By the end of 1914 seventy Territorials from Barnard Castle were on active service. In 1915 the 17th Battalion DLI was formed at Barnard Castle and lived under canvas on the Camp Field at Deerbolt, where the men were trained to join other battalions serving abroad. When the men of the 17th Battalion had to go, they were given a farewell supper on the eve of their departure and were each presented with a campaign wallet and food for the journey. There were emotional scenes when crowds of well-wishers gathered at the passenger station and at the Harmire level-crossing to cheer them on their way.

600 men from other regiments were billeted in the town in the Bowes Museum, the Witham Hall, Sunday schools, the Montalbo Hotel, the workhouse and, later, day schools while the pupils were taught in the museum. The Masonic Hall was kept in reserve in case it was needed as a fever hospital, though a fever hospital had already

The colours of the 4th Battalion Durham Light Infantry were paraded in Galgate on the 9th July 1914, before being 'laid up' in the parish church.

The 17th Battalion Durham Light Infantry leaving Barnard Castle to join other battalions on active service overseas in 1914.

been built beside the Eggleston road a few years earlier. Belgian refugees were also accommodated and money was raised to help Dutch prisoners of war. Barnard Castle gained a high reputation for its kindness to troops and refugees, often giving them entertainments and free suppers.

As the war went on, funds for soldiers' comforts began to diminish and house-to-house collections were organised. Sadly, no-one offered to collect in Thorngate or Bridgegate, so the manager of the Co-operative shops said that people could leave donations there. Food became in short supply and land was turned into vegetable plots at the County School and the Bowes Museum, and German prisoners of war worked on farms.

At last peace came, and thoughts turned to celebration and commemoration. After the South African war there had been a spontaneous torch-light procession, a town memorial was erected in one of the Galgate enclosures, and a regimental plaque was placed in the parish church. After the Great War, more circumspection was shown: the official celebrations did not take place until the 19th June 1919, when a grand organised procession passed through the town, coming to a halt to sing Handel's 'Hallelujah Chorus'. As well as official organisations, the procession included a tableau of Britannia and her allies and, in more sombre mood, an open carriage bearing three local men who had each lost a leg in the war. A film show, sports, dancing, a dinner, and fireworks and gifts for children completed a memorable day.

In 1921 a Durham Light Infantry memorial was erected on the west side of the museum park's formal garden, and in 1923 the town's own memorial was erected on the east side. It bore the names of 125 men who had died in the war, and at its official unveiling the first of many wreaths was laid by a Mrs Smith of Bridgegate, a widow

Britannia and the allied nations — a tableau forming part of the parade which, in 1919, celebrated the end of the Great War.

The main entrance to the barracks, when the buildings were used to rehouse people from unfit dwellings.

who had lost five of her six sons in the war. A large wooden and stained-glass screen with double doors was placed in the parish church as a further memorial.

As soon as the war ended, the medical officer of the Urban District Council began to emphasise the absolute necessity for a programme of rehousing the large number of people who lived in unfit conditions. In 1919 the doctor identified the Bank, Bridgegate, and Thorngate (a total area of 8.75 acres/3.5ha) as 'unhealthy' areas, and stated that 577 persons should be moved to better accommodation than that in which they were then living. No action was taken since there was no other accommodation into which 'de-housed persons' (as they were termed) could be moved. Dr. C H Welford, the medical officer, pointed out in 1920 that there was a need for 165 new houses to remedy both overcrowding and unhealthy conditions, and he and the surveyor were continuing to inspect more properties. The doctor's pleas for action became more impassioned, and in 1928 he 'earnestly begged' the council to build new houses for people living in conditions that 'were unfit and could not be made fit.' At last, in 1930, some action was taken when the council purchased the barracks, the former headquarters of the old militia which had been put into 'suspended animation' in 1920; these were adapted to provide twenty-five dwellings for people who moved from unfit houses.

Meanwhile, a voluntary 'ladies committee' was working with the medical officer and the district nurse. Health clinics helped up to 500 people a year, and up to 150 families received a visit; in total, 3,120 visits were made in 1924. Proprietary health foods and cod liver oil were sold, or in some cases freely given, and woollen clothes were distributed. The dispensary also continued its good work, and the fever hospital in Marwood Parish had room for twenty-four children or twelve adults.

One of the leading members of the ladies committee was the wife of Mr John Ingram Dawson, clerk to the Urban District Council. As a tribute to her, and to serve the cause of better health in the town, Mr Dawson built in Vane Road, at his own expense, a house for two nurses. It was occupied in 1923 and he endowed it to cover repainting and maintenance. After the National Health Service was instituted it passed into private ownership.

There was an increased sensitivity to people's needs in the 1920s. In 1922 children

The former nurses' house in Vane Road.

from the workhouse were moved into an ordinary house, 20 King Street, with a foster-mother; they attended local schools, where their neat appearance contrasted with some of the pupils who came from poor families elsewhere in the town.

From 1902 the schools that had been founded by various churches had been under the control of Durham County Council, but the Church of England and the Roman Catholic schools to a large extent kept their respective religious identities. Attendance was better, but there were still frequent absences, either condoned or deplored, and constructive outside activities for children were organised. There were cricket fixtures, and an annual Teesdale Musical Tournament, and in 1923 Mr R T Richardson gave the town a children's playing field, which by public donations was equipped with swings, a see-saw, a sand-pit, and rings suspended from a frame for gymnastic exercises.

There were three cinemas in 1924: the Victoria Hall, the Wycliffe Kinema, and the Scala

Blagrave's was a museum called the 'House of Mystery.'

in lower Galgate, said to be 'one of the prettiest cinemas for miles around'. It was the town's only purpose-built cinema. Blagrave's House, on the Bank, was adapted to be a museum, called the House of Mystery, having implements of torture, pieces of armour, antique furniture and, it was claimed, a statue of Shakespeare as a boy.

Numerous clubs were formed for both culture and sport, and the North Eastern County School, which had changed its name to Barnard Castle School in 1924, staged a demonstration game of rugby football in 1928. People came from miles around, and treated it as a comic football match and roared with laughter.

Despite all these lively activities there was a current of worry, even alarm, in the town. The Urban District Council needed more money, for the improvements to the town's sanitation had put more pressure on the water supply and, moreover, the original supply pipes were old and leaking. In periods of dry weather, the bell-man went round, ringing his hand bell and proclaiming: 'Notice is hereby given that the water will be turned off from eight o'clock at night until six in the morning, until further notice.' The signs of poverty among the people were becoming more

Raby Avenue, where, formerly, medieval soldiers paraded and Victorian footballers
played matches.

pronounced, and were giving concern to doctors and nurses. The town's heyday as a
carpet and woollen manufacturing centre was long gone; factories were derelict and
the weir beside Thorngate Wynd was broken. The other more recent manufacturing
firms did not employ nearly so many people as had once worked by the riverside, and
even Ullathornes flax mill was employing well under a third of its former workforce.
Hopes for fuller employment briefly rose when a motor car manufacturing business
began in Thorngate Mill. It produced the Black Prince Motor, a chain-driven
two-seater car with an air-cooled engine, but the firm lasted for only three years
(1919-22) before it ceased trading.

Only the upper part of the town, often referred to as 'above the Market Cross', was
continuing to thrive, and even in the market areas some aspects of the agricultural
year were diminishing. Hirings Day survived into the 1930s, but on a small scale and
in lower Galgate instead of round the Market Cross; horse sales were also conducted
in lower Galgate, but had almost died out in the face of rivalry from the internal
combustion engine. The weekly general market was, however, as flourishing as ever,
with stalls extending from the top of the cobbled area in the Horse Market to part of
the way down the Bank, with farming families still arriving by horse and trap. The
new motorised forms of transport actually increased the market's popularity when,
in 1928, Mr George H Maude pioneered a bus service which linked outlying villages
to Barnard Castle on Wednesdays. Other companies followed Mr Maude's example,
and Barnard Castle became more than ever the 'Capital of Teesdale'.

The town began to grow in size, too. The ancient Harmire Road was lined with
semi-detached houses and bungalows, with two streets at right-angles to it, and three

streets were built at right-angles to Raby Avenue, where medieval soldiers had formerly been drilled and nineteenth century footballers had played matches. A fine new Roman Catholic church was built at the corner of Birch Road and Newgate, within the Bowes Museum Park grounds but with access from the street, and in 1928 the bodies of the founders of the museum, John and Josephine Bowes, were moved from their family vault at Gibside in northern County Durham, and re-interred outside the east end of the new church. Within the former parade ground of the nearby barracks, bungalows were built for people whose homes had been demolished, and fields were acquired to the north of the barracks so that more houses could be built as the housing scheme progressed.

Poverty in the town was, however, increasing. Ullathornes Mill at Bridge End closed in 1931 because of foreign competition, putting 100 people

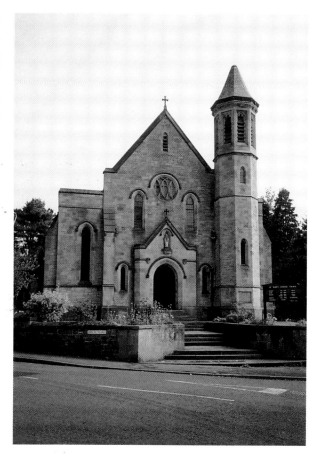

The Roman Catholic church, consecrated in 1928.

out of work, and in 1933 the brick chimney of Thorngate Factory was felled into the river, the symbol of the end of an industrial era. The boy scouts were given all the bricks which they could retrieve, and they used them in building their scout hut in the town playing-field. Within two years the North of England Chamois Leather Company had taken over Thorngate Factory and became a source of employment for nearly fifty years, but this was the only significant change in the situation in the lower part of the town. The Salvation Army took over Dunns carpet factory, adding to the help being provided by a Church mission on the Bank and a Methodist mission in Thorngate. Consideration was given to declaring Barnard Castle a 'distressed area', thus qualifying it to receive government grants to help with projects which would give employment to its inhabitants. The council, however, did not wish to gamble some of its money on drawing up plans for projects which might not be given a grant and which could not, otherwise, be afforded.

Minor schemes to make the town still more attractive to visitors were accomplished from ordinary revenue: the old spa spring which had been silted over was re-discovered, and sign posts were erected pointing the way to it through the woods; a small dam across Percy Beck made a paddling pool for children; and, most significantly of these measures, the old rubbish dump near the castle was levelled, re-turfed, and surrounded

The brick chimney of Thorngate Factory was felled into the Tees in 1933.

by seats to make the attractive 'Scar Top', which quickly became popular. The houses and shops at Amen Corner, at the junction of Newgate and the Bank, were demolished to widen the road and open up a pleasing view of the church.

Much of the council's and its officials' energy went, however, into the demolition of unfit properties in the lower part of the town and the rehousing of the occupants. At a public enquiry involving members of the Ministry of Health, the town clerk, Mr J I Dawson, said: 'I wish to pay the highest tribute to the inhabitants. The cleanliness and care taken of the premises indicates that it is not the tenants' fault that the buildings have to be condemned.' He said that the buildings were in some cases 'not equal to the majority of dwellings housing cattle'. By the end of 1937, a street of fifty-four semi-detached houses with front and back gardens had been built beside the children's playing field. The street was called Dawson Road as a tribute to the town clerk. The 'slum clearance' scheme, as it was called, was really gaining momentum, and the medical officer's report for 1938 recorded that fifty-four more houses would be built in 1939. This paragraph, however, was later amended with a neat handwritten note which reads: 'Owing to the outbreak of war, work on the scheme has been held up.'

Mr Dawson retired as town clerk in 1939; one of his last services to the town was to acquire for the Urban District Council its first permanent offices. He bought a large house called Woodleigh and gave it to the council in return for an annuity payable to him during his lifetime. Its large garden became an 'Old People's Rest Park' before being linked to the Scar Top for the use of the general public.

In the age of the motor car, many farmers still relied on horses. Horse sales and hirings days were held in lower Galgate during this period.

Barnard Castle's first official arms.
(see page 125)

Woodleigh, built as a private house, became the offices of
Barnard Castle Urban District Council.

Mr J C Walker succeeded Mr Dawson as clerk to the council. Mr Walker was
already conversant with the normal requirements of local government, but war brought
more and new challenges. They included air-raid precautions, the issue of gas masks,
food rationing, fuel rationing, and the reception and accommodation of children
evacuated to Barnard Castle from areas expected to suffer from air raids. After the
council officials had mastered the instructions issued from Whitehall, they passed on
their knowledge to various voluntary bodies who organised different aspects of the
town's wartime responsibilities. In the first year of the war they instructed 140
volunteers, and it says much for the wartime spirit of co-operation that when 400
child evacuees from Tyneside arrived in one day at the start of the war, all of them
were provided with foster-homes by nightfall.

The children were taught by their own teachers, working a shift-system with local
teachers and their pupils, but as the expected air-raids did not happen in the early
months of the war, gradually the evacuees returned to their own homes. Meanwhile,
under private arrangements, other schools stayed longer in temporary accommodation.
Boys from Middlesbrough High School, for example, were taught in the Bowes
Museum, and shared the science laboratories at Barnard Castle School.

The largest growth of population was, however, caused by turning Barnard Castle
into a military centre. Beginning in 1940, six large camps were built within three
miles (5km) of the town, the nearest being just across the river at Deerbolt. While
these camps were being built, soldiers were housed in any large buildings that were
available, including the Wycliffe Cinema, the heckling shops, the Masonic Hall, the
Co-operative Society's former shop premises in Bridgegate (the society having acquired
other premises farther up the town), and Ullathornes Mill where the men slept on

thickly-spread straw. Some were billeted in private houses, whose owners received sixpence a day per man, with a larger allowance for officers.

The camps eventually accommodated over twenty different regiments in rapid succession before being more lastingly occupied by the 54th, 59th and 61st Training Regiments of the Royal Armoured Corps. Barnard Castle became a very important military centre. Thirty special trains arrived on one day, bringing every conceivable kind of military equipment, including convoys of tanks which became famous in the annals of the war. Men who had trained on open land near Barnard Castle later played key roles in the Middle East and Normandy. Royal Engineers' equipment was brought to Barnard Castle before being used in the D-Day landings, and there was a battle school in which combat conditions were simulated with live ammunition. Two officers were killed during training at the battle school (later known as the school of infantry), and in November 1940 seven members of the South Staffordshire regiment were drowned during a sudden flood while they were engaged in a temporary bridge-building exercise on the Tees.

Many officers and government officials of the highest rank visited the area. Winston Churchill watched training at the battle school, and the headquarters train of the American army stayed for two days at Barnard Castle during tank manoeuvres on the moors, while seventy Allied generals were present, and it is highly likely that during this time the strategy of the North African campaign was fundamentally agreed. No bombs ever fell on the town or on the camps and the training areas, but it is no exaggeration to say that concerted air-raids on and near Barnard Castle would have had a very significant impact on the course of the war.

In many ways Barnard Castle gained greatly from being a military centre. All ranks regarded it as their temporary home town, and joined in and enhanced its activities. First-class cricketers regularly played on the town ground; musicians contributed to church services and to concerts in the Bowes Museum and the Victoria Hall; plays were produced in theatres on the camps, to which the public were welcomed; and dances in the Witham Hall and on Deerbolt Camp were also well attended. Economically, shops and public houses benefited greatly, and the camps continued to be in use, though on a diminished scale, for some twenty years after the war had ended.

When peace came there were spontaneous celebrations, including some street parties, but official rejoicing was deferred until the early summer of 1946, during which an immensely successful victory meet was held. But there was also the sad thought that fifty-two men would never return to their home town. Their names were later recorded on a panel added to the memorial in the museum park, and a garden of remembrance was created in the Galgate enclosure which already contained the South African War memorial.

Former features of the town were revived: the curfew rang again at eight o'clock each evening, having been suspended in wartime because the ringing of church bells was the official warning of invasion. The curfew was generally supposed to date from the twelfth century and its sound was nostalgically welcomed, though it survived for less than ten years after the war. The town band, nearing its centenary, was re-formed, and land that had been dug over during the 'Dig for Victory' campaign was restored to its peacetime use. The mood of the immediate postwar years was reflected in a spectacular outdoor production of *Merrie England* in the museum park in 1949 by a specially formed pageant society.

The council's programme of rehousing began again with renewed vigour. Plans were drawn up for 102 houses on the Station Road site, resulting in Marwood Drive

Bridgegate old and new: *(above)* about 1894, and *(below)* a modern view from
the same viewpoint.

Medieval combat in the castle ruins: an assault on the round tower; and combatants rest between bouts. *(See page 130.)*

and a continuation of Montalbo Terrace, with the name changed to Montalbo Road. There was still a waiting list of 300 applicants for council houses, so Green Lane and vacant parts of Victoria Road were used, and the adjoining streets of Hilton Road (commemorating Abraham Hilton, one of the town's nineteenth century benefactors), Greta Road and Dale Road were created. The Urban District Council in partnership with North East Housing were proceeding remarkably well, but were trying to cure rapidly a condition that had lasted for nearly 200 years.

Fortunately the problems of unemployment in the town had greatly diminished owing to the arrival of a new factory in 1944. The firm of Glaxo Laboratories Ltd needed more buildings to produce penicillin, the 'wonder drug' of the era, and by 1946 the factory was employing 450 people. Over the next fifty years, during which several other products were manufactured, the number employed by Glaxo at Barnard Castle rose to 1,800. Not all came from the town itself — some were from the surrounding area, and others were 'imported' from other Glaxo factories — but the impact on the town's economy was great, and especially appreciated by those who had known prewar conditions. Glaxo also made a significant contribution to the social life of the town. The firm gave very substantial financial help to a number of organisations and projects; and its own social club, which accepted non-employees as associate members, provided musical, sporting and theatrical events, often in co-operation with local clubs and societies.

HM the Queen Mother on her visit to the Bowes Museum to witness the transfer of trusteeship of the museum to Durham County Council.

The pageant society repeated its success with *Merrie England* and then, in 1953, the year of the queen's coronation, produced *The Yeoman of the Guard* with the castle wall as its setting and the audience on tiered seating on the Scar Top. This was not so successful, partly because of unfavourable weather and partly because the rather featureless section of the castle wall was drab compared with the 'un-English' but more attractive setting of the Bowes Museum.

The Bowes Museum was in severe financial difficulty, Victorian bequests having proved inadequate to meet modern expenditure. Admission charges were re-introduced, parts of the grounds were turned to grass instead of flower beds, and even part of the museum's collection was sold; fund-raising events were only stop-gap measures and the future was bleak indeed. The museum was rescued when, in 1956, Durham County Council took over financial responsibility for the museum and park. Queen Elizabeth the Queen Mother witnessed the formalities, having been generous in her support and having become Patron of the Friends of the Bowes Museum, an organisation formed in 1950. As a member of the Bowes-Lyon family, she was keeping alive the historic connection between the Bowes family of Streatlam Castle and the people of Barnard Castle.

The park was saved, but farm fields surrounding the town were disappearing. In 1939 private houses in Cecil Road had stopped abruptly among pastures and corn fields. In 1952 the line of the road continued up to Woodside, a development composed of military officers' houses, later inhabited by officers of a young offenders' institution at Deerbolt, created when the army camp was demolished. No longer could travellers arriving by train stroll through fields, enjoying views of the far side of Teesdale as they approached the town. The speed at which the urban area had grown was remarkable. Between 1945 and 1967, 600 council houses were built. One result, as in the nineteenth century, was a new water shortage, solved this time by linking the town to the Tees Valley and Cleveland's water supply, with a meter in an underground chamber near the Montalbo Hotel.

Comparatively few new houses were built on the site of demolished buildings; gaps on the Bank and in Thorngate were 'infilled', and Thorngate Wynd was rebuilt, but only about half of Bridgegate was built up, so the town did gain a new green area free of houses. Two old buildings survived. One was a public house and the other was an eighteenth century residence with a nineteenth century carpet factory attached. Along the rest of the street, grassy slopes were created over the rubble of the houses, mills and shops which had once crowded tightly together. Views of the river and the castle cliff which had been obscured for perhaps 400 years were revealed again.

Green spaces were retained for children's play areas in various parts of the new housing estates, and the town gained a new public garden when the Urban District Council acquired in 1958 a piece of land that formed part of the castle grounds but which had long been used as the private garden of a doctor living in the Horse Market. In 1952 the castle had passed into the control of the Ministry of Works (and, later, English Heritage) and the gardens were eventually grassed over, together with almost all the land inside the castle walls.

A number of old buildings changed their functions during this postwar period. The Starlings had been used as a military hospital in wartime, with an operating theatre and an X-ray unit, but in peacetime became a convalescent home called the Richardson Hospital. In the ensuing years it greatly expanded and became part of an area which included a health centre, with a group practice of doctors, and other buildings for people in need of help from Social Services.

The swimming pool in Teesdale
District Council's sports centre.
(see pages 128-9)

Market day has always been a lively and bustling occasion.

The completed housing scheme of Bridgegate and Thorngate Wynd.

Demolition in Bridgegate in the 1950s. The house on the left of the row and the indistinct building beyond it were the only ones to survive.

For a few years after 1958, the castle garden was a pleasant place in which to relax.

Ullathornes Mill gradually deteriorated before it was demolished in 1976.

The former mills which survived the first onslaught of demolition were used in a wide variety of ways. Dunns factory became a privately-run games and sporting club; Ullathornes Mill was occupied by a mushroom grower, a lemonade bottler and a processor of oven-ready poultry, before it was finally demolished in 1976. Its weir had long been broken but in 1962 was replaced by a modern weir, with the Urban District Council and the Water Board sharing the cost. This restored one of the town's former attractions, a view of the castle reflected in the smooth stretch of the Tees below the Water Bridge.

Much of Barnard Castle's past was recalled in the town's first official coat of arms, generously provided by Councillor Roy Watson, and formally presented to the Urban District Council by Lord Barnard in 1960. The heraldic design *(see page 115)* incorporates the Baliol shield, the castle, emblems of former owners, features of the old burgesses' seal, and the town's connection with the Bowes family. This new design replaced the burgesses' seal which had hitherto served as the town's official symbol. The motto below the coat of arms reads *'Nec temere, nec timide'* ('Neither rashly nor timidly'), the family motto of Lord Barnard. It can also be taken to express a desirable policy for local government.

Additional interest was created in the history of the town and the responsibilities of local government when in 1965 the Council for British Archaeology included Barnard Castle in a list of fifty-one towns which should be 'the direct concern of the Ministry of Housing and Local Government' because these towns 'are so splendid

The original street plan of the town can still be seen in the twentieth century.

and precious that the ultimate responsibility for them should be a national concern'. One of the criteria for inclusion as a 'Historic Town' was that the original street plan should still be recognisable and form part of the quality of the town; other criteria which applied to Barnard Castle included an ancient bridge and other buildings worthy of preservation. Within four years, much of Barnard Castle was designated a conservation area in which any inevitable changes should be made with great sensitivity to the character of the town. At first there was much local concern that this would cause undue restrictions on judging planning applications. Time has mellowed though not quite eradicated these feelings, and a realisation has grown that the object of a conservation area is to maintain elements which make a town attractive to live in and to visit.

By this time, the railways which had brought so many visitors to the town over the past century had closed. Roads had superseded rail just as, a little over 100 years earlier, the popularity of rail had caused roads to fall into disrepair. In the 1950s only two passenger trains ran to Bishop Auckland each day, and the regular users were mostly girls going to Bishop Auckland Grammar School; in 1960 a co-educational grammar technical school opened in Barnard Castle, reducing even further the number of railway passengers. The trans-Pennine line carried goods traffic in the 1950s, but proposals were already being made to cut the passenger service, and the last train passed over Stainmore in 1962. The beautiful route to Middleton-in-Teesdale was closed in 1964 to passengers and in 1965 to goods trains. The great viaduct which had given travellers impressive views as they crossed high over the Tees was demolished in 1972. The sound of the explosions as its stone pillars were blown apart could be heard in the middle of the town, and signalled the end of an era.

In 1974 Barnard Castle lost an institution that, unlike the railway, was still central to the life of the town: in a national re-organisation of local government, the Urban District Council ceased to exist, being superseded by a new administrative body

The Tees Valley railway viaduct was demolished in 1972.

Councillors and officials of Barnard Castle's last Urban District Council in Woodleigh Gardens in 1973. *Back row, left to right*: J Mitchell (Deputy Clerk), F Duffy, F P Murton, M G C W Wheeler, J R Hinchcliffe, Dr A S M Wilson (Medical Officer), Mrs D P Dodds, A E Stoker, E Dixon (Public Health Officer and Surveyor). *Front row*: A Wilkinson, N Jackson, J C Walker (Clerk), R Watson, J Barker, E T Close, G A Carter.

called Teesdale District Council. Effectively this meant that the town no longer ran its own affairs. It is true that since 1888 Durham County Council had been the higher level of local government, but the Urban District Council had continued to have direct control over most aspects of urban conditions. It had been responsible for surfacing and lighting all streets and pathways in the town, except for classified roads which passed through Barnard Castle and were the responsibility of the county council; the Urban District Council carried out its own scheme of drainage and sewerage until it was taken over by the Northumbrian Water Board; the council conducted its own system of refuse collection and disposal, and the maintenance of public lawns and gardens, footbridges, seats and paths in Flatts Woods; its officers inspected meat and food preparation, slaughter houses, shops, factories, offices, hotels and boarding houses; it was responsible for the upkeep of car parks and public lavatories, organising allotments, and the demolition of dangerous structures, and had powers of compulsory purchase. Even when the regional housing association became the agency for the actual building of council houses, the selecting of tenants remained the responsibility of the council. Planning applications were considered by the Urban District Council and recommendations were passed on to the county council, which gave its approval to almost all of them.

Under the new arrangement, all these duties passed into the control of Teesdale District Council, whose authority extended from upper Teesdale down to Gainford and northwards to the borders of Weardale. There had been twelve Urban District

Councillors, whereas now the town had only six representatives on the new Teesdale District Council, on which they were outnumbered by approximately five to one. Members and officials of the former council had been well known to most of the inhabitants of the town, but the great majority of the new district councillors lived elsewhere, and very few people knew who they or their officials were.

It is not too much to say that the trend of Barnard Castle's history had been reversed. The Baliols had given charters to the town and encouraged self-government; this had led to the Borough Court, the Vestry, the Board of Health and, in 1894, the Urban District Council. Now, in 1974, the management of the town had largely been taken away from the townspeople.

At this point both Mr J C Walker, the clerk to the Urban District Council, and Mr E Dixon, who combined the posts of public health inspector and surveyor, retired. Mr Walker, a native of the town, had been on the council staff for forty-six years, and Mr Dixon had served for twenty-nine years. Their intimate knowledge of the town and its people had been invaluable.

The newly-created town council, with its chairman holding the title of town mayor, had the status of a parish council, and after some uncertainty about what its duties should be, undertook some minor responsibilities such as providing Christmas lights, flower baskets, managing children's playing fields on behalf of the owners, the National Playing Fields Association, and placing plaques on historic buildings. With growing confidence, it then began to restore to public use the Witham Hall which had largely been taken over by a private business concern. This proved to be expensive and difficult, but the council supplied materials, a government-sponsored Task Force supplied labour, and Durham County Council's architect supplied technical advice. When the hall opened in 1981 as a communal social and sporting centre for Barnard Castle and district, it was run by the YMCA which had been active in the town since 1940. Within a few years the YMCA ceased to operate and its funds were left in trust to be used in the future in any way approved by the national governing body. The Witham Hall was then run by a community association with help from Durham County and the town council, which held the lease.

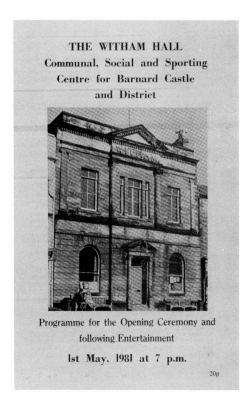

THE WITHAM HALL
Communal, Social and Sporting Centre for Barnard Castle and District

Programme for the Opening Ceremony and following Entertainment

1st May, 1981 at 7 p.m.

20p

The front of the programme celebrating the re-opening of the Witham Testimonial as a public amenity in 1981.

Within ten years of the opening of the Witham Hall, the town's and Teesdale's amenities were greatly enhanced when the district council opened the Teesdale Sports Centre in Barnard Castle, providing two sports halls, two squash courts, a swimming pool and a toddlers' pool, and two tennis courts outside the building. It was perhaps the swimming pool which gave the most general satisfaction, for it was something which had been discussed for at least sixty years; a self-replenishing swimming pool in the Tees had, in fact, been proposed as one of the projects to attract government grants in the 1930s when Barnard Castle was a 'distressed area,' but nothing had come of it.

The creation of the sports centre could not have been achieved by Teesdale District Council alone, and considerable help was given by Glaxo, who contributed £250,000 — the biggest contribution ever given by the firm to a community project in the United Kingdom. The firm had prospered in Barnard Castle, and its factory buildings — in a variety of architectural styles — had by this time extended into the surrounding countryside, from which the buildings were later screened by belts of trees.

The Glaxo buildings from the north.

While these new buildings were being created, older ones in the town were being adapted or restored. Teesdale District Council sensitively re-developed into flats the two former Methodist churches and their adjoining buildings in Broadgates and the old Ranters Yard, which was more respectfully renamed West View. More good work of a similar kind was done by a society called the Teesdale Buildings Preservation Trust, which bought old buildings and turned them into modern residences while preserving their original outward appearance. The money raised from the sale of the restored property was then used to repeat the process with another building.

The mechanics institute committee transformed its outdated reading room into a modern art gallery for exhibitions by individual artists or groups, including

A weavers' house in Thorngate restored by the Teesdale Buildings Preservation Trust.

schoolchildren, and old venues for theatrical performances were revived by an amateur dramatic company called the Castle Players, which used the castle and then the Bowes Museum and Park as settings for a series of lively productions of Shakespeare's plays.

Anniversaries of notable events in the town's past were celebrated during the last decades of the twentieth century. On the 150th anniversary of Charles Dickens' visit, a stagecoach conveyed the novelist's great-great grandson, Mr Christopher Dickens, from Greta Bridge to Barnard Castle, despite being held up by 'highwaymen'. Mr Dickens was then driven to Bowes, where he met Mr Edwin Shaw, the great-great grandson of William Shaw, who is generally accepted to have been the schoolmaster whom Dickens depicted as the proprietor of the fictitious Dotheboys Hall. Other features of the anniversary included townspeople in period costume, and there were lectures and readings from the novels. Four years later, in 1992, the centenary of the first opening of the Bowes Museum was celebrated with an imaginative carnival parade in which groups of performers represented items in the museum's collection; a masque was performed on the terrace, and the evening concluded with fireworks and impressive lighting effects from the windows of the museum itself.

Those were special events, but visitors and residents regularly enjoyed children's fun days and band concerts on the Scar Top, and falconry, jousting and medieval battles in the castle. Barnard Castle continued to be a popular holiday resort for day tourists or for those staying for a week or two in the town or elsewhere in Teesdale. Numerous houses offered accommodation and catering, and in 1997 the Tourist Information Centre, organised in Woodleigh by Teesdale District Council, was visited by 29,670 people. In the same period 60,504 people looked round the Bowes Museum and, between April 1996 and April 1997, the castle had 27,288 visitors. The customary Barnard Castle Meet, changed from Whitsuntide to the weekend of the Spring Bank Holiday, was still a feature of the year, despite almost annual fears that the tradition was coming to an end.

Inevitably, time did bring some changes to the town. The spread of new housing extended well beyond the former town boundaries, though it did not much increase the population, which was 4,779 in 1991, only about 200 more than it had been a century earlier. Instead, the town centre became much less residential as flats above the shops and business premises were left empty. Traffic conditions became more crowded as more people drove into the town centre to work or for shopping, and the ancient streets vibrated to the roar of heavy goods vehicles, many of them having no business in the town but simply passing through to other destinations.

The old County Bridge was closed to heavy traffic, but when the Abbey Bridge was used as a substitute, vehicles came along Newgate and their efforts to turn at right-angles round the Market Cross were both dangerous and destructive. There were long discussions on the need for a town bypass. A provisional route was chosen, which many people feared would spoil the beauty and tranquillity of the woods. In any case, Durham County Council announced that no bypass would be created before the twenty-first century. This temporarily allayed the fears of those who were worried about the effect of a bypass on trade.

The market itself had shrunk since the prewar days; even the cobbled area had diminished in size since the early years of the century. As in other market towns, the

Two costumed 'highwaymen' hold up the coach conveying Mr Christopher Dickens along the route taken by his famous ancestor in 1838.

Barnard Castle
Meet, 1989: the
town band leads
the procession; a
Roman tableau by
girl guides and
brownies; and
riders of antique
cycles recall the
origins of the meet.

The Horse Market in 1992; heavy traffic creates difficulties in the ancient street.

market had also become a quieter place: no longer was it attended by entertainers such as the mind-readers and escapologists who in the 1930s had performed on the cobbles, when several of the stallholders, too, had been an entertainment in themselves. They had belonged to a more leisurely age when people seemed to have more time to stop and stare, and they had been replaced by a more serious or inhibited generation.

Market day continued, however, to be a lively and bustling occasion. The cattle market had been in Vere Road (the former Flatts Lane) for 100 years and held an exhibition to celebrate the centenary. The covered pens and ring directly behind Galgate were derelict, but the original buildings in the field beside Vere Road were still in use. Some of the structure was modernised but the rest was beginning to show its age. Modern cattle wagons were finding difficulties in negotiating the narrow streets and parked cars, and there was talk of moving the cattle market out of town. If this were to happen, an important aspect of life in Barnard Castle would go.

However, as the end of the twentieth century approached, the town still maintained its ancient function of providing shops, services and markets for a large surrounding area. That is what had always ensured its survival after the castle, which had led to the town's creation, was abandoned. Religious, military, and industrial influences had all played a part in modifying its life and moulding its features until, from being a feudal settlement, Barnard Castle had become a modern town without losing its historic qualities.

Two views of the Market Place: early in the twentieth century; and in the 1990s.

A calf sale at the auction mart.

The lower Demesnes — shown here — and the upper Demesnes are still freely used 'for exercise and pleasure'.

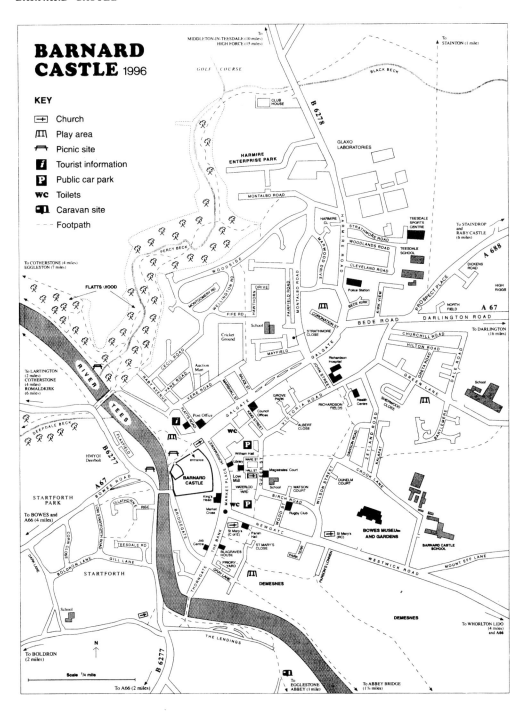

Based upon Ordnance Survey material with the permission of the Controller of Her Majesty's Stationery Office, © Crown Copyright Licence No MC85365M.

It is fortunate in still having on its outskirts the open spaces created by the Baliols in the twelfth century. To the east lie the upper and lower Demesnes: there have been some minor intrusions onto the ancient land in the form of allotments and rugby pitches, but the Demesnes are still 'constantly open to the inhabitants for exercise and pleasure.' To the west of the town, the former hunting park is still a constant source of woodland beauty.

The preservation of visible history within the town is a matter for conservationists and planners. In 1995 a further forty of the town's buildings, including houses, stables, memorials, a dovecote, public houses and a bank, were 'listed' as being of historic and architectural interest. A total of well over 200 structures thus receive a considerable measure of protection for the future.

This, if combined with sensitive local government and a lively community spirit among the town's inhabitants, will continue to justify the words which greet travellers who arrive over the County Bridge:

'Barnard Castle, historic market town.'

Sources

Anon, *A History of the Darlington and Barnard Castle Railway, by An inhabitant of Barnard Castle*, 1877.

Anon, *Barnard Castle in War Paint, A Stationmaster's Diary*, c1945.

Anon, *Illustrated Guide to Teesdale and District*, Published by Chorley and Pickersgill, 1900.

Anon, *The Universal British Directory*, 1792.

Atkinson, R W, *The Durham Militia*, 1869; enlarged edition 1884.

Atkinson, W R, *Penny Guide to Barnard Castle and District*, c1902.

Atkinson, Frank, *Life and Tradition in Northumberland and Durham*, 1986.

Austin, D, *English Heritage Guide to Barnard Castle*, 1988.

Bogg, Edmund, *The Wilder Borderland of Richmondshire*, 1909.

Boyle, J R, *A Comparative Guide to the County of Durham*, 1892.

Buckrose, J E, *Rambles in the North Yorkshire Dales*, 1913.

Burgess, John, *A History of Three Valleys*, 1989.

Carr, Jean and Gavin, *Barnard Castle Methodist Church Centenary*, 1994.

Carroll, Lewis, *Diaries* (ed Roger Lancelyn Green), 1954.

Charnley, Emerson, *An Account of the Great Floods in 1771 and 1815*, 1818.

Clarke, Rev Blackburn, *Lays of Castle Barnard*, 1908.

Clifton, T, *A Tour in Teesdale*, 1828.

Coggins, Denis (ed), *People and Patterns, the carpet weaving industry in 19th century Barnard Castle*, 1996.

Dawson, J Ingram, *Reminiscences of a Rascally Lawyer*, 1949.

Defoe, Daniel, *A Tour through the Whole Island of Great Britain*, 1726.

Fordyce, William, *The History and Antiquities of the County Palatinate of Durham*, 1855-57.

Garland, R, *A Tour in Teesdale*, 1804.

Grose, *Antiquities of England and Wales*, 1775.

Hardy, C E, *John Bowes and the Bowes Museum*, 1970.
   Barnard Castle School; a Centenary Book (ed with K C N G King and A Wilkinson), 1983.

Heavisides, M, *Rambles by the River Tees*, 1905.

Hitchcock, R C, *The History of Barnard Castle School, 1883-1933*, 1933.

Hutchinson, William, *History and Antiquities of the County Palatine of Durham*, 1794.

Jones, R J, *Barnard Castle Parish Church*, manuscript of 1913, printed 1993.

Layton, G, *Castle-Barnard, a poem*, 1823.

Leland, John, *Itinerary* (ed T Hearne), 1770.

Mackenzie and Ross, *The County Palatine of Durham*, 1834.

Macquoid, Katherine, *About Yorkshire*, c1882.

Page, W (ed), *Victoria County History, Durham*, 1907.

Pearson, W, and White, W, *Durham and Northumberland*, 1827.

Pinnock, *The History and Topography of Durham*, c1820.

Pocock, D, and Norris, R, *A History of County Durham*, 1990.

Ramsden, Allen, *A Guide to Places of Interest and Beauty*, 1920.

Ramsden, D M, *From Stainmore to the Tees*, 1948.
  Teesdale, 1947.

Ranger, William, *Report to the General Board of Health on the Township of Barnard Castle*, 1850.

Richardson, M A, *Local Historian's Table Book*, 1846.

Sharpe, Sir Cuthbert, *Memorials of the Rebellion of 1569*, 1840.

Smisson, Rev E A, *The Way We Have Come*, 1936.

Smith, Norma L, *William Smith & Sons, a Family Business*, 1991.

Sopwith, Thomas, *An Account of the Mining District of Alston Moor, Weardale and Teesdale*, 1833.

Stobbs, Allan W, *Memories of the LNER South West Durham*, 1989.

Steele, Anthony, *History of Methodism in Barnard Castle and the principle places in the Dales Circuit*, 1857.

Surtees, Robert, *History and Antiquities of the County Palatine of Durham*, 1814.

Sykes, John, *Local Records*, 1866.

Waistell, Doris, *Barnard Castle Thoughts*, 1962.

Ward, M J, *An Excursionist's Guide*, c1890.

Watson, Nigel, *Glaxo at Barnard Castle: a Celebration*, 1994.

Wesley, John, *Journal* (ed Nehemiah Curnock), 1914.

Whellan, Francis, *History, Topography and Directory of the County Palatine of Durham*, 1894.

White, J W, and Wayne, W, *The Jubilee of the Barnard Castle Co-operative Society Ltd*, 1912.

Wilkinson, Alan, *Barnard Castle in Old Picture Post Cards, Volume I*, 1983.
  Volume II, 1990.
  100 Years of Barnard Castle Meet, 1979.

Articles in Periodicals and Collections

(i) Durham County Local History Society Bulletin
Barke, M, 'Migration into Darlington in the mid-eighteenth Century', *No 27*, 1981.

Ellison, L, 'Petty Crime in Barnard Castle in the late nineteenth century', *No 27*, 1981.

Milburn, Geoffrey, 'Reading between the lines: Some thoughts on Wesley's *Journal*', *No 42*, 1989.

Smith, H J, 'The Teesdale Workhouse Paternity Case', *No 46*, 1991.

(ii) in other publications
Chapman, Vera, 'Barnard Castle, the Town and the Enclosures' (from *History Field Studies in the Durham Area*), 1967.

Hemingway, Jean, 'Benjamin Hepworth, building contractor of Barnard Castle' (from *Journal of the Teesdale Record Society*), 1993.

Medlam, Sarah, 'A Sawmill in the 1920s' (from *Regional Furniture*, vol V), 1991.

Proctor, H G, 'History of Man in Teesdale' (from *Natural History of Upper Teesdale*), 1965.

(iii) newspapers, etc

Files of the *Darlington and Stockton Times, Northern Echo, Teesdale Mercury,* and issues for 1994 of *In Touch, the Glaxo Barnard Castle Staff Magazine.*

Select List of Unpublished Records and other Material

Photographs and transcripts of the medieval charters. Private Collection.

Surveyors' book for the township (eighteenth century). Durham County Record Office (DCRO).

Minute book of the Open and Select Vestries (eighteenth/nineteenth century). DCRO.

Proceedings of the Local Board of Health (nineteenth century). DCRO.

Minutes of the Urban District Council (nineteenth/twentieth century). DCRO.

Proceedings of the manor court (nineteenth century). DCRO.

Photographic collection with miscellaneous writings by Fred Nevison, local historian (nineteenth/twentieth century). The Bowes Museum, Barnard Castle.

Log books of the National school, Wesleyan day school, Church of England and Council schools (nineteenth/twentieth century). DCRO.

Records of Durham Militia (nineteenth/twentieth century). Durham Light Infantry Museum, Aykley Heads, Durham.

Proceedings of Barnard Castle and Startforth Rural District Councils (twentieth century). DCRO.

Annual reports of the medical officer (twentieth century). DCRO.

List of non-ecclesiastical charities (twentieth century). Private Collection.

Newsletters of Middlesbrough High School evacuees (twentieth century). Private Collection

Background Reading

(a) local

Coggins, Denis, *Teesdale in Old Photographs,* 1989.

Kay, Martin, (ed), *The County Durham Book,* 1973.

Pevsner, N, *The Buildings of England: County Durham,* 1953.

Raine, Parkin, *Teesdale (a second selection) in old photographs,* 1994.

Thorold, Henry, *Shell Guide: County Durham,* 1980.

(b) general

Hibbert, Christopher, *The Story of England,* 1992.

Kenyon, J P, *Dictionary of British History,* 1981.

Richardson, John, *The Local Historian's Encyclopedia,* 1974.

Ridley, Jasper, *The History of England,* 1981.

Trevelyan, G M, *English Social History,* 1942.

Index

Illustrations are listed in **bold**.